country style

for the home

country style
for the home

Inspirational and practical decorating
projects for the home

STEWART AND SALLY WALTON

LORENZ BOOKS

This edition is published by Lorenz Books

Lorenz Books is an imprint of Anness Publishing Ltd
Hermes House, 88–89 Blackfriars Road, London SE1
8HA
tel. 020 7401 2077; fax 020 7633 9499
www.lorenzbooks.com; info@anness.com

© Anness Publishing Ltd 1998, 2003

This edition distributed in the UK by The Manning
Partnership Ltd, 6 The Old Dairy,
Melcombe Road, Bath BA2 3LR;
tel. 01225 478 444; fax 01225 478 440;
sales@manning-partnership.co.uk

This edition distributed in the USA and Canada by
National Book Network,
 4501 Forbes Boulevard, Suite 200, Lanham, MD 20706;
tel. 301 459 3366; fax 301 429 5746;
www.nbnbooks.com

This edition distributed in Australia by Pan Macmillan
Australia, Level 18, St Martins Tower,
31 Market St, Sydney, NSW 2000;
tel. 1300 135 113; fax 1300 135 103; customer.serv-
ice@macmillan.com.au

A CIP catalogue record for this book is available from the
British Library.

Publisher: Joanna Lorenz
Project Editor: Clare Nicholson
Designer: Lisa Tai
Photography: Graham Rae
Step-by-step photography: Mark Wood
Additional Photography: Michelle Garrett, Lizzie Orme
Stylist: Leean Mackenzie

Previously published as *Creating Country Style*

10 9 8 7 6 5 4 3 2 1

Contents

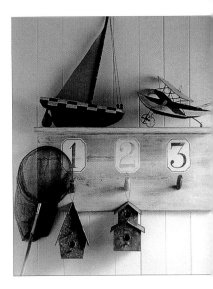

Introduction

Decorating in the country style is a way of saying "Welcome", as clearly as if the word was written on your doormat. It sends out a subliminal message to everyone who enters, inviting them to kick off their shoes and put on a comfortable (but stylish!) pair of slippers. Perhaps the best part is that the actual process of creating is so much fun. Take your time and enjoy it – even the simplest projects should not be rushed. We hope that you will treat this book in the same way, exploring the first chapter and absorbing the basics, then browsing through all the different ideas before choosing the one you most fancy as your first project.

Right: A selection of wonderfully tactile country pieces, all hand-crafted in the traditional way.

Creating Country Style

You do not have to live in the countryside in order to want to decorate your home in the country style. People who live in rural areas are often less likely to seek a deliberate country look than those of us who live in towns and cities, where we feel a strong pull towards the romantic country idyll. In our imaginary countryside, fields of corn rustle in the breeze, farmers still drive horse-drawn vehicles and wonderful smells of home baking waft from the kitchen of our dreams.

The country look has come to mean assembling and embellishing a mixture of handmade things that we no longer have the time or space to make for ourselves. Hand-hooked rugs, perfectly stitched quilts, knitting, embroidery and appliqué work soften the hard edges of wooden benches and stools. Some country-style furniture is quite rough and

ready, but it combines comfortably with loved and polished antiques. It is the essence of a home evolving over many years, with no need to rush.

The lifestyle still exists, as if time has stood still, in some closed communities such as that of the Amish, who have the time to sew their famous quilts by hand, keeping everything plain in accordance with their beliefs. They still manage to combine breathtaking colours with exquisite simplicity to make some of the most sought-after textiles and fabrics in the world. The Shakers were also inspired by religion and

Above: These painted panels have been treated with antiquing wax.

Left: Clever use of tongue-and-groove and cream paint gives these ordinary shelves a kitchen dresser look.

Above: The rustic furniture combines with the wall striping and stamping to give this hallway a Mexican country look.

now, 200 years later, almost everything they designed is revered, copied and becoming very fashionable.

Country decorating has no hard edges, colour schemes are mellow and textures are natural – comfort is paramount. New pieces of furniture sit well alongside the old as long as the colours and style are in harmony. Furniture made from reclaimed wood is very popular these days. It has the weathered, worn appeal of old timber combined with the stability and strength of something newly crafted. We recommend reclaimed timber for the furniture projects in this book.

Use it rough, with all the pitting and raised grain patterns, or plane and sand it to a smooth finish then polish with antiquing wax. This is a tinted beeswax that mellows the colour of the wood, leaving a deep sheen.

To choose fabrics with a country look, take your inspiration from quilts, rugs, tapestries and weaving. Checks, ginghams, plaids and small floral patterns are all in the country mood, as are stripes and plain fabrics in earthy or plant-dyed colours. Look at nature's colours – the colours of rust, straw, earth and pebbles, set off against a clear blue sky.

Try to see the familiar things around you in a new light. Look at the pattern on an old china plate or the colours in a favourite picture. Each time you take your inspiration from the objects you love to have around you in your home, you reinforce your own individual style. And every time you make something with your hands the experience is enriching.

Quiet concentration is refreshing as well as rewarding. We hope you will find inspiration within these pages to take the time and enjoy the projects as much as we did.

Country Palette

The country palette is rich and varied, drawing on all the natural colours that we can see around us throughout the seasons. Think of the icy greens, blues and greys of winter, the iridescent spring greens that replace them, then the riot of summer colours followed by the rich, mellow shades of autumn. This is the country palette, but it would not be advisable to throw the whole lot in together – a limited palette is the key to success.

One way to decide your colour schemes is to take them from a painting, quilt or piece of china with a definite country look that holds a particular appeal for you. Painted walls suit the look, especially when the paint is applied as a colourwash. This will give a mottled patchy effect, like dappled sunlight rather than a regular all-over coating. Colour washing is the best background to use for stencilled or stamped patterns and particularly complements any uneven texture in the wall. It is also the ideal way to build up strong, rich tones by laying one colour over another. Try mixing your own colours, following the paint mix instructions below. This country-style colour range is designed to harmonize with antiques, natural building materials and old textiles.

Key to picture

1 Cadmium Red Light and Yellow Ochre (equal parts)
2 Cadmium Red Light
3 Cadmium Red Deep and Venetian Red (equal parts)
4 Burnt Sienna and Venetian Red (equal parts)
5 Chromium Oxide Green x 4 and Raw Sienna x 1
6 Hookers Green x 2 and Yellow Ochre x 1
7 Cobalt Blue x 3; Burnt Umber x 1; White x 1
8 Ultramarine x 2; White x 2; Raw Umber x 1
9 Raw Sienna
10 Yellow Ochre and Golden Ochre (equal parts)
11 Yellow Ochre and White (equal parts)
12 White x 6; Raw Umber x 1

Above: *This chequerboard floor design uses contrasting terracotta and green – perfect colours to remind us of the countryside. A combing technique has been used to vary the intensity of the colours and allow the wood grain to show through.*

Country Textures

The textures of textiles, such as rough and homespun cloth, sacking, woven rugs and soft knitted woollen shawls, all conjure up the comfort of a country home. Wood that is smooth planed and sanded or worn from years of use is what we expect inside the house, and weathered and bleached bare wood or peeling, naturally distressed painted wood outside.

Handmade pots with natural earth colours and glazes sit comfortably alongside the cool smoothness of decorative china pieces on a wooden shelf. Cast iron hinges and handles on painted tongue-and-groove doors provide a real contrast in textures, especially once the iron has become pitted with age.

Floors of worn flagstones or floorboards reveal paths most trodden, but if you cannot wait for this to happen naturally a bit of clever fakery with antiquing varnish and moulded resin flagstones will provide the visual effect. The country look is utilitarian, without too many fussy frills and flounces, but there is room for pretty textural contrasts in the bedroom with cotton quilts, embroidered cushions and crisply starched bed linen.

Above: *Pierced tinware looks good in a country kitchen, and this heart-shaped platter has acquired a wonderful patina with age. Combined like this, in a group with earthenware mugs and sheaves of wheat, the effect is stunning.*

Left: *A wrought-iron strap hinge supporting a painted plank door. The pitted iron against the wood provides a real contrast in textures.*

Top left: *A clever use of chicken wire. This little hanging container has been made by bending chicken wire around a wire frame.*

Bottom left: *An unusual contemporary country appliqué, using a woven background to set off a bird with a button eye.*

Right: *The texture of this hand-thrown ceramic pot sits well against the simple, plain wall surface.*

Country Materials

In the last century, before the railway arrived, all building was done with local materials. So, if you lived somewhere that had a good supply of brick, stone, timber or flint, then this is what your house was made from.

Country materials come from natural sources – trees, plants, animals and the earth, but these days a lot of the goods we buy will have been manufactured in factories that have little connection with the countryside. Luckily, most country people still think locally when it comes to materials, and it is always a joy to discover a local basket weaver, wood carver or potter selling their wares in markets or at country fairs.

Choose textiles woven from wool, flax or cotton, and go for the ones

Right: Natural dyes and roughspun cotton give these Shaker-style fabrics a warm homespun quality.

Below left: Stir up summer memories with a basket filled with dried cottage garden flowers.

Below right: Reels of intensely coloured paper twine are perfect for tying up bunches of herbs or flowers. Using twine instead of string will make all the difference to a display.

Top left: *Old kitchen implements such as wooden spoons and rolling pins should be snapped up to add authentic touches to the contemporary country kitchen.*

Top right: *A simple tin star, made into something special by hammering a dented but not pierced pattern into the back. A group of different shapes makes an eye-catching display.*

Below: *Handmade and naturally dyed papers bound together with rough twisted twine.*

with irregularities rather than smooth perfection. Loose woven or knitted throws can be used to soften chairs, hooked rag rugs are a very economical way to dispose of old clothes and gain a warm treat underfoot. Wood always feels warm, and is best oiled and beeswaxed to bring out the grain and add a delicious aroma. Quarry tiles are practical and good-looking for kitchen floors, and their warm colour suits the country palette. When in doubt always choose natural over synthetic and local over imported, and you will not go far wrong.

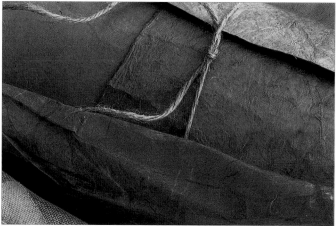

Motifs and Patterns

ome patterns used in country-style decorating are inspired by nature and the country life-style; flowers, the sun, trees, farm animals and birds all feature. Others have come from traditional sources like the heart, which always stands for love, or the star, which appears more in American country style than European but is a universal motif because we all live beneath the stars.

Plaid patterns and checks are a result of the weaving process. When all fabric was handmade on a loom, some threads were coloured with nat-ural dyes made from the earth, berries and roots and then interwoven with the undyed threads. We associate the classic cream and red, blue, green or yellow checks and stripes with this style. Nowadays, when there is such a great range of patterns available, there is something particularly comforting about choosing these simple basic patterns and colour combinations for our homes.

In the same way that the weaving process limited the way cloth was patterned, most country motifs have been simplified to suit their method of

Left: *The classic geometric eight-pointed star, used here as a stencilled border but seen more often as a pieced quilt pattern.*

Above: *The pineapple was used to convey hospitality, so this stamped pineapple is the ideal motif for a placemat on the dinner table.*

Right: *This border has been hand painted on to floorboards, using a stencil for the basic shape and adding details freehand.*

Above: *The heart is one of the most popular motifs in folk art and country decorating. Its meaning as a love symbol is universally understood.*

Below: *These beautiful hand-stitched quilts have been made with traditional patterns. The basket is a symbol of generosity; the pineapples mean hospitality.*

Above: *This breakfast tablecloth is decorated with a geometric cockerel motif. It is a traditional country farmhouse motif that reminds us of the early morning.*

production. Stencils pare down motifs, concentrating the main characteristics of each shape so that it can be cut and painted effectively. Each cut-out section of a stencil needs a "bridge" to keep it attached to the rest of the design, and these give stencilled patterns and motifs their distinctive look.

Stamped patterns have a similar "cut-out" quality to stencils, but they have no bridges to interfere with basic shapes. Country painters are not slaves to convention though, and it is common to find a mixture of techniques used on a wall or piece of furniture – a simple stencilled leaf shape, for instance, with freehand veining added with the sweep of a brush.

You find the same applies in patchwork quilting and appliqué, where shapes are cut and sewn, or in tapestry and cross stitch, where the silks are worked on to a mesh backing, which makes all motifs more angular.

When looking for country motifs and patterns, choose anything that celebrates nature's bounty – sheaves of wheat, fruit, farmhouses, barns, weather vanes, farm gates, cows, sheep, horses, dogs and cats, a cockerel, geese and wild birds, traditional patterns such as stars, hearts, baskets, checks, stripes and bows. All of these can be interpreted in many different ways to create wonderful patterns in your home.

Surfaces

One of the things you notice first in a country home is that the interior decoration places equal emphasis on comfort and practicality. If people are likely to walk mud through the hall, there is no point laying a pale carpet or hanging expensive wallpaper. Instead floors are polished wood or flagstone and walls are panelled or painted. Mellowed or distressed paintwork immediately fits in with existing country furnishings and will accept wear and tear quite amiably. In this chapter we focus on interesting ways to paint interior surfaces – walls, floors and woodwork – in true country style.

Right: *Pigments and stains can be stirred into easy-to-use water-based paints to create your own country colour schemes.*

Country Surfaces

Country style should appear effortless and look as if it has always been there. This may sound difficult at first, but a few basic techniques will give you the confidence to relax and enjoy this very "hands on" approach to decorating your home.

The wall finishes most associated with the country look are colourwash, chalky distemper, limewash, stencilling, stippling and distressing. Colourwash is often used as the base for further decorative effects such as stencilling. When paint is washed on to a wall, it makes it appear dappled with light and shade, and even the smoothest modern wall takes on a more interesting surface texture.

Country woodwork is left natural, perhaps with a coat of varnish, or painted with matt (flat) paint, not gloss. Emulsion (latex) paint is often used on bare wood then sanded off to reveal the grain beneath. Fine-grade wire wool (steel wool) can be used

instead of sandpaper – it is less scratchy and gives a smoother finish. Another simple technique is to run a candle along the edge of a skirting board or other piece of woodwork, then apply a water-based paint over it. The wax resists the paint, giving the effect of natural wear and tear.

Stencils can be bought ready-cut, and many companies send out mail-order catalogues of their designs. You

can also cut your own designs from stencil card (cardboard) or plastic. This way you can decide on the size of the design and tailor it to suit your room, and it is much more satisfying to go through the whole process yourself – the sense of achievement is well worth the extra effort. For an unusual effect, try the Star Stencil project, in which we show how to stencil a wall with varnish, something we discoverd

Above: The stencilling here has been done with a very light touch to blend with the mottled and dragged backgrounds. The crisp perfection of the bed linen provides a strong contrast.

Left: A contemporary kitchen with new units and appliances is softened by adding a diluted wash of mottled colour to the walls.

Above: This is formal country style with a Scandinavian theme. The flat blue background has been stamped with two similar motifs to create a dynamic background for the elegant mirrors.

by accident one day when we splashed varnish on a painted wall.

Stamping produces a similar result to stencilling, but by the opposite method. Instead of working with a negative (the cut-away part of the stencil) you use a positive (the actual stamp), which is inked and pressed on to the surface. Stamps can be made out of foam rubber, erasers, kitchen sponges or polystyrene (styrafoam). The Horse Border is done with a stamp. As with stencils, many mail-order companies and shops now supply readymade stamps in a wide variety of designs.

All the surface finishes shown in this chapter are simple and satisfying to do. They provide the perfect background for country-style furniture and accessories.

Gingham Painted wall

Gingham is, of course, the classic country-style fabric, but here this perennial favourite has been given a fresh new twist by imitating it in paint. The clever but simple technique is to cut the paint roller in half so that you can paint two stripes at the same time. For a completely different effect, try using the traditional Shaker pattern of brick red checks on a buff background.

YOU WILL NEED

- **white emulsion (latex) paint**
- **large decorator's paintbrush**
- **small foam paint roller (as sold for gloss paint)**
- **masking tape**
- **craft knife**
- **yellow emulsion (latex) paint**
- **small sponge**
- **spirit (carpenter's) level**

1 *Paint the walls with white emulsion (latex) as a base coat. Wrap a piece of masking tape around the centre of the foam part of the paint roller.*

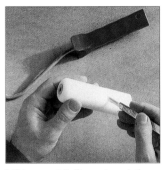

2 *Using a craft knife, cut through the foam, using the edges of the masking tape as a guide on either side.*

3 *Peel off the masking tape with the foam attached, to leave a space in the middle. Reassemble the paint roller.*

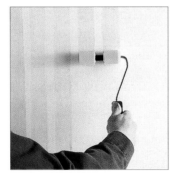

4 *Fill the paint tray with yellow emulsion (latex) and run the paint roller through it. Starting as close to the top of the wall as possible, paint even vertical stripes. Fill in any gaps at the top or bottom with a small sponge. Leave to dry.*

5 *Paint the horizontal stripes, using a spirit (carpenter's) level to keep them straight. Focus your eyes on a point ahead and your arm will then naturally follow in a straight line.*

Star Stencil

This misty blue colour scheme is ideal for a bathroom or staircase because the lower part of the wall is varnished to provide a practical wipe-clean surface. The tinted varnish deepens the colour and gives it a sheen that contrasts beautifully with the chalky distemper above. The stencil is a traditional quilting motif.

YOU WILL NEED

- star template (see page 150)
- tracing paper and pencil
- scissors
- spray mount adhesive
- stencil card (cardboard)
- sharp craft knife and cutting mat
- soft blue distemper or chalk-based paint
- large decorator's paintbrushes
- straightedge and spirit (carpenter's) level
- clear satin water-based varnish
- Prussian blue artist's acrylic paint

1 *Trace the star shape and cut out. Spray the back lightly with adhesive, then stick it on to the stencil card (cardboard).*

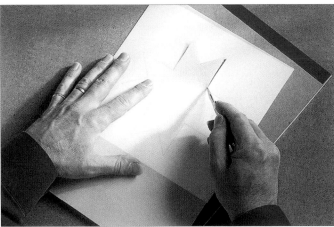

2 *Using a craft knife, cut out the star. Cut inwards from the points towards the centre so that the points stay crisp.*

➤

3 *Peel away the paper template to reveal the stencil.*

4 ▷ *Dilute the paint, if necessary, according to the manufacturer's instructions. Brush it on to the wall with sweeping, random strokes to give a colourwashed effect.*

5 ◁ *Using a straightedge and spirit (carpenter's) level, draw a pencil line across the wall at the height you want to end the varnished surface.*

6 ▷ *Tint the varnish with a squeeze of Prussian blue acrylic paint. Using a separate brush, apply this on the lower part of the wall up to the marked line.*

7 ◁ *Spray the back of the stencil lightly with adhesive and position at one end of the wall, about 5 cm (2 in) above the marked line. Stencil with the tinted varnish, using a broad sweep of the brush. Repeat along the wall, spacing the stars evenly.*

Country Wall surface

✳ Tongue-and-groove is a typical wall treatment in country cottages, larders and pantries, especially when topped with a display shelf for a collection of pretty china. Tongue-and-groove is practical as well as decorative, providing insulation and hiding uneven surfaces. Another advantage is that it is simple to hammer nails into the wood if you want to hang pictures. Most timber merchants and hardware stores sell tongue-and-groove, sometimes even in kit form.

YOU WILL NEED

- **retractable tape measure**
- **straightedge and spirit (carpenter's) level**
- **three lengths of battening, to fit your wall width**
- **hand drill**
- **wall plugs (plastic anchors)**
- **screwdriver and screws**
- **tongue-and-groove planks, to fit your wall depth – measured from skirting board (baseboard) to picture-rail height**
- **hammer**
- **panel pins (small fine nails)**
- **fine nail punch**
- **shelf brackets, enough to fit your wall width when spaced 60 cm (24 in) apart**
- **15 cm (6 in) wide shelving plank, to fit your wall width**
- **flat beading (molding), to fit your wall width**
- **saw**
- **white emulsion (latex) paint**
- **medium decorator's brush**

1 *Carefully remove any existing skirting board (baseboard), to be replaced later. Using the straightedge and spirit (carpenter's) level, mark the position for three levels of battening at the top, centre and bottom of the wall. Drill and insert the wall plugs (plastic anchors), then screw the battens in place.*

2 *Place the first tongue-and-groove plank against the wall and attach to the three battens with panel pins (nails). Check the vertical with the spirit (carpenter's) level. Tap panel pins (nails) through the inside edge of the "tongue" into the battens.*

3▷ *Using a nail punch, hammer the heads of the panel pins below the surface of the wood.*

➤

4 *Drill holes 60 cm (24 in) apart for the shelf supports so that the shelf will sit at the top of the tongue-and-groove. Screw in place, checking that they are level.*

5 *Place the shelving plank on top of the brackets. Drill holes to line up with the brackets, then screw in place from above.*

6 *Cut a piece of beading (molding) to fit between each pair of brackets. Tap in place to conceal the raw edges of the tongue-and-groove. Replace the skirting board. Paint the tongue-and-groove and shelf with white emulsion (latex) diluted 50/50 with water.*

Painted Staircase

Painting a staircase in three strong colours makes it into a central feature that will transform a room. For a co-ordinated look, repeat the colours on the walls. Gloss paint is normally used on stairs because it gives a thick, tough surface, but when it begins to chip off it looks very scruffy. Here ordinary emulsion (latex) has been used instead, painted over white primer. You can also paint directly on to bare wood – when the paint wears, the wood will show through to give the distressed finish so typical of country style.

YOU WILL NEED
- **white acrylic primer**
- **emulsion (latex) paint: soft blue, mustard yellow and brick red**
- **medium and small decorator's paintbrushes**
- **dust sheet (tarp)**
- **masking tape**

1 *Paint the wooden staircase with white acrylic primer. Paint the wall behind the staircase with blue emulsion (latex), continuing the colour a quarter of the way across the stair treads and risers. This edge will be painted over.*

2 *Paint the banisters and side panel with mustard yellow emulsion (latex). Protect the rest of the staircase and floor with a dust sheet (tarp).*

3 *Paint the outer skirting with blue emulsion (latex), continuing the colour a quarter of the way across the stair treads and risers as in step 1.*

4 *Place strips of masking tape down the staircase, leaving an equal amount of blue paint either side. Paint the centre of the treads and risers with brick red emulsion (latex). Paint the handrail brick red, leave to dry, then add a thin yellow line.*

Stamped Horse border

✹ Add extra interest to a painted floor or wall with this simple border pattern. Cutting the stamp isn't difficult but works best if you use high-density foam, the type used for camping and exercise mats. Don't attempt to cut right through the foam the first time. Use a small paint roller to apply the paint – if you simply press the stamp into the paint, it will absorb too much. Practise first on paper before starting the border. It's very easy!

YOU WILL NEED
- **hired sanding machine and hand-held electric sander (for unpainted floors)**
- **horse template (see page 150)**
- **tracing paper and pencil**
- **spray mount adhesive**
- **square of 1 cm (½ in) thick high-density foam**
- **craft knife**
- **ruler**
- **wood stain: light blue and white**
- **medium decorator's paintbrush**
- **dark blue emulsion (latex) paint**
- **small gloss paint roller and tray**
- **clear matt (flat) hardwearing polyurethane varnish and brush**

1 *If your floor is unpainted, sand with a hired sanding machine, then finish with a hand-held electric sander.*

2 *Trace the horse motif. Spray the back lightly with adhesive, then stick it on to the piece of foam.*

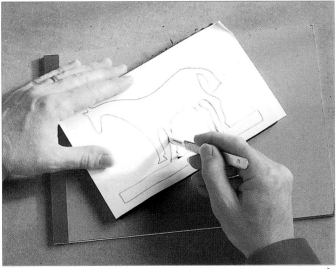

3 ▷ *Using a craft knife, "draw" a cut around the horse. Correct any sharp angles.*

➤

4 *Make another angled cut to meet the first, then pull away a thin strip of foam from the edge of the horse, revealing the outline. Cut through the full depth of foam. Peel off the paper.*

5▷ *Place the stamp on the floor to help determine the width of the border, a little way out from the wall.*

6◁ *Paint the thin strip of floor near the wall with blue wood stain. When dry, paint the border area with white wood stain. Stain the rest of the floor blue.*

7▷ *Pour some dark blue emulsion (latex) into a paint tray. Using a roller, apply an even coat of paint to the stamp.*

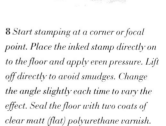

8 *Start stamping at a corner or focal point. Place the inked stamp directly on to the floor and apply even pressure. Lift off directly to avoid smudges. Change the angle slightly each time to vary the effect. Seal the floor with two coats of clear matt (flat) polyurethane varnish.*

Chequerboard Floor

✻ Painting a patterned floor may seem a daunting task, but stunning results such as this combed design will bring you endless compliments. The materials cost very little compared to laying a carpet. If the room is large, use a straight-edge to check the grid lines. A cardboard square the actual size of the finished squares will also help you to align the design. Start painting in the farthest corner and paint your way out of the room.

YOU WILL NEED
- several pieces of thick mounting (mat) board
- craft knife
- white emulsion (latex) paint
- large decorator's brush
- retractable tape measure
- 2.5 cm (1 in) wide masking tape
- long straightedge (optional)
- 38 cm (15 in) card (cardboard) square (optional)
- artist's acrylic paint: terracotta and green
- medium decorator's paintbrush
- clear matt (flat) hardwearing polyurethane varnish and brush

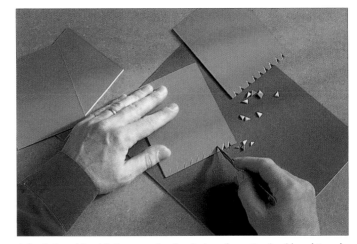

1 *Cut V-shaped "teeth" along one edge of each piece of mounting (mat) board, to make combs. The combs will soften with use.*

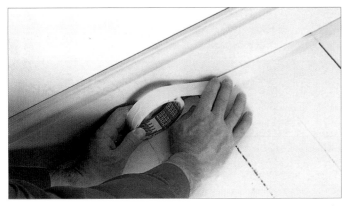

2 *Paint the floor with white emulsion (latex). When dry, lay masking tape all around the edge of the room.*

3 *Using a tape measure, mark 40 cm (16 in) squares on the tape. Start in the most visible corner, measuring half a square (20 cm/8 in) in each direction.*

➤

4 ◁ *Lay down a grid of tape lines. Use a straightedge and/or a 38 cm (15 in) card (cardboard) square, if necessary, to help keep the squares even.*

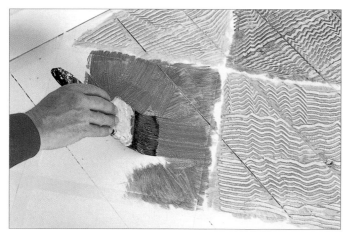

5 *Experiment on a piece of card (cardboard) to find the amount of paint most suitable for combing. Apply the paint generously on the floor, alternating the colours.*

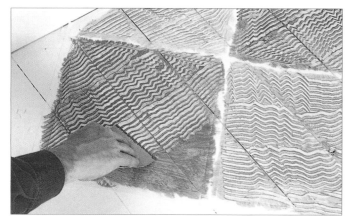

6 *Press a comb down into the paint, wiggling it from side to side to vary the pattern. Wipe off the paint when the comb begins to clog and replace with a new comb when necessary. Leave to dry overnight, then remove the tape. Apply two coats of varnish.*

Door panel Motifs

✹ These bold circles are reminiscent of the "hex" signs that the early Pennsylvanian Dutch settlers painted on the sides of their barns to ward off evil and protect the grain within. The geometric designs are drawn with a compass. You need a steady hand to paint in the colours, and it helps to use your spare hand as a support, either by holding your wrist or by resting one hand on the other.

YOU WILL NEED

- sage green emulsion (latex) paint
- medium decorator's paintbrushes
- pair of compasses
- pencil
- artist's acrylic paints: burnt umber, white, cadmium yellow and Indian red
- 1 cm (½ in) square-tipped paintbrush
- masking tape (optional)
- fine-tipped no. 2 lining brush
- clear matt (flat) or satin acrylic varnish

1 *Paint the door with sage green emulsion (latex). Using a pair of compasses and pencil, draw two large circles in the centre of each top panel.*

2 *Keeping the same radius measurement, draw the stylized petals. Place the compass point on the edge of the circle and make a series of arcs as shown.*

3 *Add smaller circles as shown, using the compass.*

4 ▷ *Mix a little burnt umber into some white acrylic paint. Fill in the panels, painting around the circles.*

➤

5 *Using the square-tipped paintbrush, paint the door beading (molding) yellow. Use masking tape to give a neat edge, if you find it difficult.*

6 △ *Using a fine-tipped no. 2 lining brush, carefully fill in the petal shapes in each circle. Then leave to dry.*

7 *Fill in the red dots.*

8 △ *Edge the yellow beading (molding) with fine red lines. Leave to dry, then varnish, using a separate brush.*

Painted Window surround

❋ This window treatment is inspired by pargeting, a traditional technique in which wet plaster was imprinted with simple patterns. This painted version, with mock panels on either side, would make a feature of an awkward window. Experiment with thinning the paint – it should flow smoothly off the brush. Instead of a painter's mahl stick (maulstick), you can tape a small wad of cotton wool covered with lint or chamois leather to the end of a stick.

You will need

- **white emulsion (latex) paint**
- **artist's acrylic paints: yellow ochre and burnt umber**
- **large decorator's paintbrush**
- **ruler and pencil**
- **straightedge**
- **pair of compasses**
- **mahl stick (maul stick)**
- **no. 8 soft watercolour brush**

1 *Tint some white emulsion (latex) with yellow ochre to make a soft straw yellow. Top up with water to make a thin, milky glaze. Brush on to the wall, varying the direction of your strokes to give an uneven colour.*

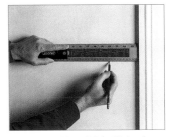

2 *Measure a 10 cm (4 in) wide border around the window, using a straightedge, and draw in lightly in pencil.*

3 *Leave a gap of 15 cm (6 in), then draw a panel on either side of the window. The width of the panel should be half the width of your window. Draw a 10 cm (4 in) border inside each panel.*

4▷ *Using a pair of compasses, draw two circles inside each panel. Draw quarter-circles in the corners.*

➤

5 *Practise holding the mahl stick (maul stick) against the wall with your spare hand to support your painting hand. Mix some burnt umber into the paint, then paint over the border outlines.*

6 *Add the diamond shapes freehand, painting stripes first in one direction and then the other.*

7 *Allow the brush to create the corner motifs. Touch the point of the brush down, then splay it out as you curve into the corner.*

8 *Add smooth curves to each circle, to represent stylized wheel spokes.*

9 *Fill in the panels with diagonal stripes.*

Furniture

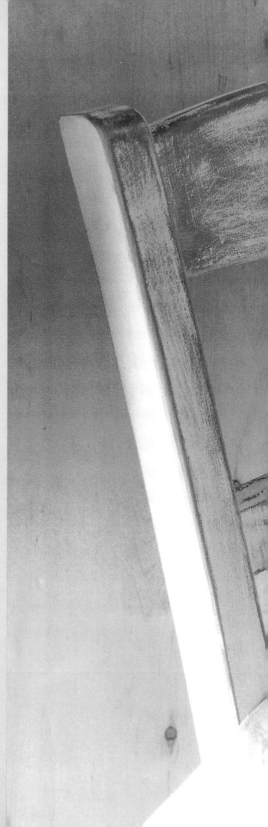

Country homes usually contain a mixture of old and new furniture, with a strong emphasis on handmade and family pieces. You can give an old wooden chair an instant new look simply by adding a colourful knitted cushion or embroidered backrest, and there is natural continuity in living this way.

Don't worry if you have no family heirlooms – the painted furniture you produce today will become the family heirlooms of tomorrow.

Right: This pretty kitchen chair has been given the lime-washed look by painting it matt white and then rubbing back the dry paint with fine wire wool (steel wool) to reveal some of the wood and leave a soft, chalky finish.

Country Furniture

ountry furniture was usually made of locally available wood, from trees that grew in the area or recycled wood from buildings that had fallen into disrepair. Recycling timber has recently come back into fashion, partly for ecological reasons and also because country antiques have become rare and therefore expensive. One way to furnish your home is to make your own furniture from old pine floorboards and other reclaimed household timber. Leave the finish deliberately rustic, with just a coat of matt (flat) paintwork to capture the warmth of genuine old country pieces.

Look out for old cupboards and chairs that you can revitalize with painted decoration. Many different styles and techniques are shown here,

including a beautiful Scandinavian flower design that is a complete contrast to the simple "pawprint" pattern. Simple upholstery and a lick of paint is enough to transform the Tartan Upholstered Stool.

If you are working with an old piece of furniture, you may want to strip off the existing layers of paint or varnish first. You will find that this alters the wood by raising the grain. Make a feature of this by sanding back to reveal the bare wood, but leaving some paint or varnish in the grain. In the Peg Rail project, very dilute white emulsion (latex) is applied to bare wood to give the impression of limewashed or sunbleached wood.

Whatever project you choose, consider it a good result if you add

something of yourself to the finished piece. This could be the way you allow the brushstrokes to show, your choice of colours or the uncertainty of your lining technique. The way *you* do it will give a personal charm, which is what country style is all about.

Above: *The blue and white plates make a bold display on the dresser, and the natural wooden worktop looks beautiful next to the deep glossy blue paintwork.*

Left: *The mouldings of these panelled doors give this freehand painting a formal, framed quality.*

Above: *The quirkiness and individuality of country furniture is typified by this charming chair back.*

Left: *This unusual grandfather clock was made from a rich mix of old and new timber fitted with an antique clock face. Notice how the bench alongside it has developed a rich sheen over many years of use.*

Below: *A small church pew, not built for comfort but just right for a kitchen or conservatory corner.*

Bronze C h a i r

⭐ This handsome design was inspired by the high-quality chairs produced in America in the 19th century, which would have been kept in bedrooms out of general use. This style of chair is named "Hitchcock" after the man who mass-produced them. The brilliance of the gold comes from real gold powder (or bronze powder, which is cheaper), and the effect is quite different to gold paint or gold leaf. The original makers used the finest velvet to apply the powder, moulding the shapes of fruit and flowers by varying the amount of powder.

YOU WILL NEED

- kitchen chair with broad rails and turned legs (or plain pine rocking chair)
- fine-grade sandpaper
- soft cloth
- black emulsion (latex) paint
- small decorator's paintbrush
- stencil pattern (see page 150)
- spray mount adhesive
- stencil card (cardboard)
- sharp craft knife and cutting mat
- water-based gold size
- old plate
- stencil brush
- bronze or gold powder
- square of lint or velvet
- no. 3 artist's paintbrush
- antiquing varnish (or clear satin varnish) and brush

1 *Rub down any existing paintwork with sandpaper.*

2 *Dust off the surface with a cloth.*

3 *Paint the chair with black emulsion (latex).*

4▷ *Photocopy the stencil pattern, enlarging it to fit your chair back. Spray the back of the pattern with adhesive and stick it on to stencil card (cardboard). Using a craft knife, begin to cut out the small shapes.*

➤

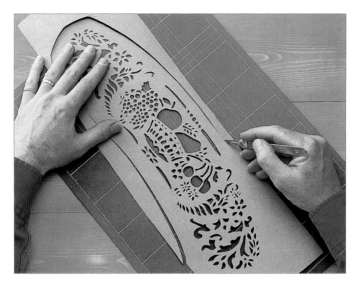

5 ◁ *Complete cutting out the pattern, then cut away the extra card (cardboard) so that the stencil fits your chair back. Lay the stencil in position on the chair back.*

6 ▽ *Place a small amount of size on a plate. Using a stencil brush, stipple the size through the stencil shapes. Use the size sparingly, but fill in each shape.*

7 *When the size is just tacky (see manu-facturer's instructions), dust on bronze or gold powder. Work it into the size by applying it with a piece of lint or velvet.*

8 ▷ *Leave the powder for 1-2 hours to set. Wipe away any excess.*

9 ◁ *Highlight details on the rest of the chair – apply size with a paintbrush, then add the bronze or gold powder.*

10 ▷ *If desired, you can soften the gold effect with a coat of antiquing varnish, which will also protect the stencilling. Clear satin varnish will give protection without dulling the gold.*

Chicken wire Cupboard

❈ Chicken wire gives a rustic look and is very practical in a larder or kitchen. The deep red paintwork is covered with a darker glaze that is combed while it is still wet. Combing is a traditional technique, popular with folk artists and country furniture makers. This style is full of vitality, so be bold and enjoy making patterns. Choose a cupboard with a panelled wooden door. It's easy to tap away any beading (molding) around each panel, then tap around the edge of the panel to free it from the door. For a professional finish, cover the edges of the chicken wire with narrow, flat beading.

YOU WILL NEED

• small wooden cupboard with panelled door
• medium-grade and fine-grade sandpaper
• acrylic paints: deep red, raw umber and ultramarine
• medium decorator's paintbrushes
• craft knife and cutting mat
• small piece of mounting (mat) board or firm card (cardboard)
• old white plate and old knife or spatula, for mixing
• PVA (white) glue
• antiquing varnish
• tape measure
• 12 mm (½ in) chicken wire
• wire-cutters
• small hammer and small staples *or* staple gun

1 *Remove the door panels and then sand over all the woodwork with medium-grade sandpaper.*

2 *Sand the cupboard again, using fine-grade sandpaper.*

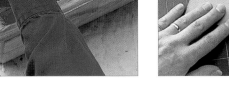

3 ◁ *Paint the cupboard inside and out with deep red acrylic paint.*

4 ▽ *Using a craft knife, cut small V-shaped "teeth" along one edge of the mounting (mat) board or card (cardboard) to make the comb.*

➤

5 *Mix a purple-brown, using all three colours. Mix this with the same amount of PVA (white) glue to make a glaze.*

6▷ *Using a separate brush, brush the glaze over the deep red paint. Comb it before the glue becomes tacky. Wipe the comb clean each time you lift it.*

7◁ *The glaze looks milky when wet but will dry clear. When the glaze is dry, apply a coat of antiquing varnish, again using a separate brush.*

8▷ *Measure each door panel, adding 2.5 cm (1 in) all round. Cut chicken wire to fit. Trim any sharp edges.*

9◁ *Using a hammer and staples (or a staple gun), staple the wire to the back of the door. Start by stapling one long side, then one end. Pull the wire taut, then staple the other two sides.*

Scandinavian Door panels

❋ Painted furniture is very popular in Scandinavia, especially designs celebrating nature. These beautiful panels are painted freehand, with flowing brushstrokes. Don't worry too much about making the doors symmetrical – it is more important that the painting should look natural. Practise the strokes with both brushes first on a piece of paper until you feel confident. Any cupboard or dresser doors would be suitable for this design, even modern kitchen units.

You will need
- **pale yellow emulsion (latex) paint –** **ochre rather than lemon**
- **medium decorator's paintbrush**
- **plant and flowerpot design (see page 152)**
- **pencil**
- **artist's acrylic paint: yellow ochre, ultramarine and white**
- **old white plates**
- **no. 3 lining brush**
- **no. 8 rounded watercolour brush**
- **clear matt (flat) varnish and brush**

1 *Paint the door panels with pale yellow emulsion (latex). Leave to dry. Draw the design on each panel in pencil, using the design as a guide.*

2 *Put some yellow ochre artist's acrylic paint on to a plate. Mix in ultramarine to make grey-green. Using the lining brush, begin painting the design at the top of the first panel.*

3 *Work your way down the panel, resting your painting hand on your spare hand to keep it steady.*

4 *Put some white artist's acrylic paint on to a plate. Mix in yellow ochre to make a light cream. Using the watercolour brush, paint the flowerpot and swirls below. Add the flowers, applying pressure to the brush. Darken the paint with more yellow ochre, then add the soil.*

5 *Paint the other panel and leave to dry. Apply a protective coat of clear matt (flat) varnish.*

Painted Wooden box

A hundred years ago country folk kept their papers and valuables locked in wooden boxes such as this. Most homes would have had several boxes and chests, in different sizes. The leaf design is painted freehand on to the lightly sanded wood. Have the pattern in front of you and follow it as a guide, but do not trace it, otherwise the painting will not flow naturally. Rubbing down the newly painted lines with fine wire wool (steel wool) helps to blend them with the old wood.

YOU WILL NEED

- **old wooden box**
- **fine-grade sandpaper**
- **artist's acrylic paint in black**
- **medium (no. 5) watercolour brush**
- **fine (no. 1) watercolour brush**
- **fine wire wool (steel wool)**
- **antiquing wax**

1 *Rub down the box lightly with sandpaper to remove any varnish or polish from the surface.*

2 *Thin the paint with a little water. Using the medium brush, paint large wavy lines for the stems. It is easier to paint a flowing line if you use your other hand as a support.*

3 *Place your spare hand flat on the box, and use it to rest on. Add leaf shapes to the stems.*

4 *Using the fine brush, add small strokes to fringe each leaf. Leave to dry.*

5 *Rub down the design with wire wool (steel wool), using enough pressure to gently distress the painted lines without lifting them completely.*

6 *Polish the box with antiquing wax, using a soft cloth.*

Limewashed Peg rail

✳ Sort out family clutter with this clearly numbered system of brightly coloured pegs. The wood for the shelf and backing board is reclaimed timber, painted with a wash of diluted white emulsion (latex) to give a limewashed effect that allows the grain to show through. The pegs are offcuts (scraps) whittled with a penknife to give a rustic look. The numerals were inspired by the enamel house numbers you see in France.

You will need

- 60 cm x 25 cm (24 in x 10 in) piece of old pine, 1 cm (½ in) thick, for the backing board
- hand drill
- three offcuts (scraps) of wood, each 10 cm (4 in) long
- penknife
- 60 cm x 16.5 cm (24 in x 6½ in) piece of old pine, 1 cm (½ in) thick, for the shelf
- screws
- white emulsion (latex) paint
- large decorator's paintbrush
- wire wool (steel wool)
- craft knife and cutting mat
- 9 cm x 11 cm (3½ in x 4½ in) piece of thin card (cardboard)
- pencil
- number templates (see page 152)
- ruler
- masking tape
- transfer paper (carbon paper)
- artist's acrylic paint: green, yellow and red
- old plate or saucer
- no. 3 artist's lining brush
- 2.5 cm (1 in) square-tipped artist's paintbrush
- wood glue
- clear matt (flat) varnish and brush *or* clear wax polish and cloth

1 *Drill three evenly spaced holes 7.5 cm (3 in) from the bottom edge of the larger piece of pine at an angle of about 40 degrees. Whittle the three offcuts (scraps) with a penknife to make the pegs, tapering one end to fit into each hole. Assemble the peg board by drilling holes and screwing the shelf into the backing board. Paint the peg board and pegs with white emulsion (latex) diluted 50/50 with water.*

2 *Using wire wool (steel wool), rub the paint to reveal the grain of the wood.*

3 *Using a craft knife and cutting mat, cut the corners off the piece of card (cardboard) as shown.*

4 Using the card (cardboard) as a template, draw three outlines in pencil on the backing board, centred above each peg hole.

5 ▷ Fill in the three outlines with undiluted white emulsion (latex).

6 Photocopy the number templates, enlarging them to 7.5 cm (3in) high.

7 ▷ Using masking tape, attach a number on top of each white outline, then slip a piece of transfer paper (carbon paper) underneath.

8 ◁ Trace around the outline of each number in pencil. Remove the templates and transfer paper (carbon paper).

9 ▷ Paint each number a different colour, using a lining brush. Practise using the brush first – it helps to support your hand to keep it steady.

10 *Using the square-tipped paintbrush, paint each peg to match the corresponding number. Glue the pegs in position.*

11 *Rub back the painted numbers lightly with wire wool (steel wool). Apply a coat of clear varnish or clear wax polish.*

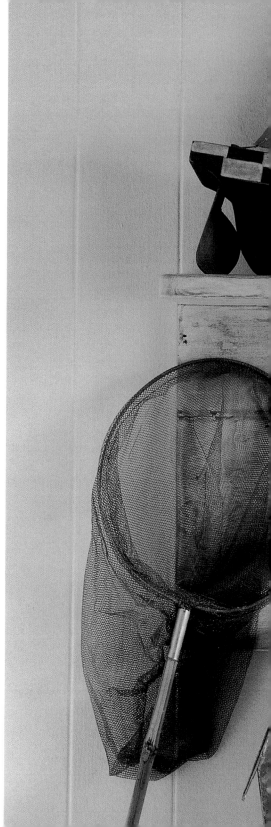

Pawprint S h e l v e s

✳ This simple paint effect is based on the traditional "pawprint" pattern – the more naive and informal it looks, the better. The decoration is applied very simply with a piece of sponge to give an all-over, random effect. This technique could be used on another piece of wooden furniture, such as a cupboard or chair.

YOU WILL NEED

- old wooden shelf unit
- fine-grade sandpaper
- acrylic paint: golden ochre and
  Venetian red
- old white plate
- small decorator's brushes
- small piece of sea sponge
- pencil
- no. 2 lining brush
- PVA (white) glue

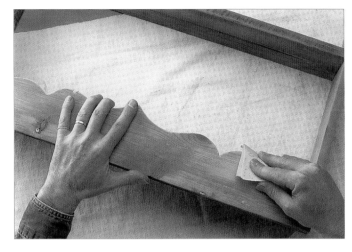

1▷ *Sand the shelf unit.*

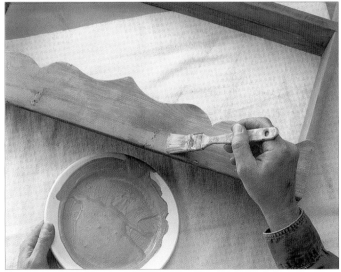

2◁ *Pour some golden ochre paint on to a plate. Paint the shelf unit and then leave to dry.*

3 *Add some Venetian red paint to darken the colour. Dip a small piece of sponge in the mixture and apply in spots all over the shelf unit. Leave to dry.*

➤

4 *Using a pencil, mark a line all around the top of the shelf unit. Rest the point of the pencil on the front, keeping your other fingers rigid, then run the pencil along to give an even line.*

5 ▷ *Using a lining brush, carefully go over the pencil line with Venetian red paint. Support your painting hand to keep it steady. Leave to dry.*

6 *Pour some PVA (white) glue on to a plate and mix in a brushful of Venetian red paint to make a slightly tinted glaze. The glue is milky when wet but will be clear when dry.*

7 ▷ *Using a separate brush, paint the glaze over the shelf unit. There is no need to varnish as the glue will protect the surface.*

Tartan S t o o l

Simple upholstery such as this is much easier since the invention of glue guns and staple guns. Once you have mastered the technique shown here, you can move on to more ambitious projects. This project would work equally well on an upholstered chair seat. Give a favourite piece of furniture the tartan treatment, or look out for an old stool in a junk shop. If the woodwork is not painted, paint it first with a white emulsion (latex) undercoat.

You will need
- **upholstered stool**
- **medium-grade sandpaper**
- **emulsion (latex) paint in a colour to match your tartan fabric**
- **small decorator's paintbrush**
- **tartan fabric, to fit the upholstered stool top plus 2.5 cm (1in) all round – the fabric should not be too thick**
- **staple gun**
- **four upholstery nails**
- **hammer**
- **scissors**
- **glue gun and glue sticks**
- **upholstery braid, to fit around the bottom of the stool top plus 2.5 cm (1 in)**

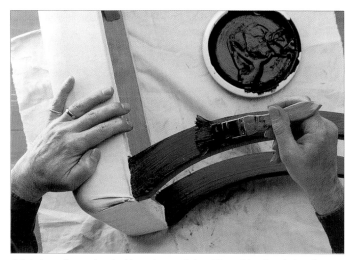

1 Rub down the woodwork with sandpaper. Paint with emulsion (latex), then drag over a dry paintbrush while the paint is still wet.

2 Place the tartan fabric centrally over the upholstered stool top. Using a staple gun, put a single staple in the centre of one long side. Pull the fabric taut, then staple the opposite side in the same way.

3 Staple the two short sides in the same way. The fabric will now be held in place by four staples.

4 Staple along the edge of each side, placing the row of staples close together. Leave the corners open.

➤

5 *Mitre the fabric at the corners and flatten the folds. Secure each corner temporarily with an upholstery nail.*

6 *Trim the excess fabric, leaving just enough to turn under a small hem and cover the corners.*

7 *Staple one mitred corner flat, turning under the small hem as you go. Remove the upholstery nail. Repeat with the opposite corner, then complete the other two corners.*

8 *Heat the glue gun. Glue one end of the braid to the bottom of the stool top at one corner. Spread a line of glue along the bottom edge.*

9 *Holding the braid taut in one hand, smooth it on to the glued line with the other hand, keeping the line straight. Fold under the end of the braid at the last corner to make a neat join.*

Kitchen Clock

✳ Every country kitchen needs a traditional wall clock, and this design also incorporates a shelf for herbs and spices. If you wish, you can decorate the simple clock case with folk art borders handpainted in bright colours. Making your own clock isn't difficult. Clock faces and movements can be bought from many places that do repairs. Cut the circular opening to fit your clock face, getting the help of a local carpenter if you don't have the necessary tools.

1 *Make the clock case, following the diagram on page 151. Paint with yellow ochre emulsion (latex) and leave to dry.*

2 *Rub in a generous coat of antiquing wax, working it well into the corners and grain (if you are using pine). Rub down the polish with wire wool (steel wool) so that the colour shows through stronger in some areas but the wax remains in the grooves and corners.*

3 *Rub the clock face with antiquing wax to mellow the colour.*

4 *Fit the clock movement to the face from behind.*

5 *Press the hands on to the spindle. Using a glue gun, stick the clock face to the inside of the case – mark the vertical centre point on the back of the clock face to help you position the numbers.*

Fabrics

Country fabrics are natural rather than man-made – muslin, calico, canvas, textured homespun linen and, of course, cotton. Floral prints, stripes, checks and plaids complement country furniture and surfaces perfectly. The tradition of making patchwork quilts and rag rugs continues today, sometimes giving a new interpretation to an old design. Appliqué, cross stitch embroidery, knitting and quilting are all part of the country style – all made with love and made to last. Create a nostalgic country mood by using a range of fabrics that are full of associations with nature and folklore.

Right: Gingham checks, striped cottons and chequered bed-spreads all improve with age. This pile of country fabrics looks far too good to hide away in a cupboard. Folded and stacked on open shelves, household linens make an appealing display.

Country Fabrics

The country fabrics that we recognize today are a cultural blend of patterns and designs from many different parts of the world. The overall country look combines the warm generosity of places such as Provence, Tuscany and Greece with the simplicity of the Shaker and Amish communities, plus a dash of medieval, Celtic and oriental spice. The unifying factor is that all these fabrics were originally made and decorated by hand, even if today they are printed and produced in factories.

In this chapter, we use a potato to print an all-over pattern on the Clover Leaf Tablecloth and a piece of sponge to print a traditional appliqué design on the Stamped Throw. Both are done with water-based inks, which are much more pleasant to work with than oil-based inks.

The sewing projects include a quick-and-easy Squared Patchwork Quilt, stitched on a sewing machine, and a hand-stitched Appliqué Window Quilt. The hand-stitching is far more time-consuming but it is very satisfying and relaxing to do, and the irregularity of the stitched outlines adds greatly to the quilt's charm. Iron-on wadding (batting) makes the whole business of making up a quilt much quicker and simpler than it used to be.

The Hooked Rag Rug is the traditional family way to pass the long winter's evenings, and a wonderful way to recycle old clothes. Another unusual floor covering is the Stars-and-Stripes Floor Cloth, made of painted canvas. Given several coats of varnish, these floor cloths are incredibly hardwearing. If you have never worked a sewing machine or tried

Above: Try embroidering simple waffle-weave cotton tea towels. This tea towel has been embellished with a Danish-style cross motif.

Left: Woven stripes in coarse cotton make ideal upholstery fabric for a whole range of country furnishings.

Above: *Stripes used horizontally instead of vertically can make narrow windows appear wider. Any fabric left over from new curtains can be used for chair skirts or cushions for a co-ordinated look.*

your hand at embroidery before, several ideas in this chapter are very simple. The Cross Stitch Napkins is an ideal project to start with.

Colours do not always have to co-ordinate because country style is often an eclectic mix of patterns and colours. Fabrics and patterns are often more appealing when they have faded over time, and the aim should be to re-create this warm, comfortable and, above all, practical look.

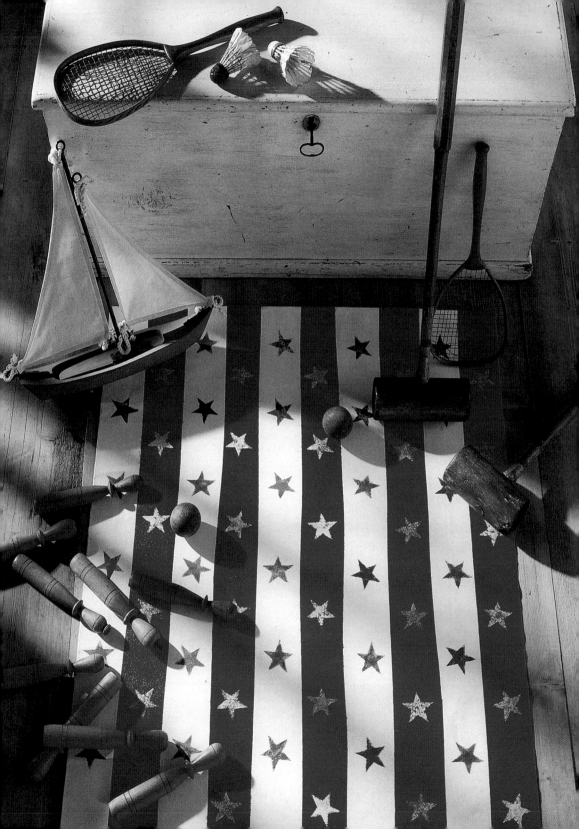

Stars and stripes Floor cloth

✳ Varnished floor cloths were introduced by the early American settlers, who recycled the canvas sails that had carried them to the New World and painted them to imitate European carpets. Make this bright floor cloth to cover most of the room or just as a small mat – artist's suppliers sell canvas in a wide range of sizes. It is available pre-primed or you can prime it yourself. Each coat of varnish you apply will add years to the floor cloth's life.

YOU WILL NEED
- natural-coloured artist's canvas, size as required
- ruler and pencil
- craft knife
- 5 cm (2 in) double-sided carpet tape
- white acrylic primer (optional)
- medium decorator's brush
- masking tape
- acrylic paint: scarlet, cobalt blue and white
- old white plate
- star template (see page 153)
- tracing paper and pencil
- spray mount adhesive
- stencil card (cardboard)
- cutting mat
- stencil brush
- clear or antique tinted matt (flat) polyurethane varnish and brush

1 *Draw a 10 cm (4 in) border on all four sides of the back of the canvas. Using a craft knife, cut across the corners as shown.*

2 *Stick double-sided tape along the border line. Peel off the backing, then fold over the raw edge.*

3 *If your canvas is unprimed, apply two coats of acrylic primer.*

4 *Mark vertical stripes 7.5 cm (3 in) wide down the canvas. Outline alternating stripes with masking tape.*

5 *Paint alternating stripes with scarlet acrylic paint.*

➤

6 *Leave to dry, then peel off the masking tape.*

7▽ *Trace the star template. Spray the back lightly with adhesive and stick on to stencil card (cardboard). On a cutting mat, cut out the template.*

8◁ *Place the stencil on a white stripe, about 5 cm (2 in) from one end of the canvas. Using a stencil brush, apply blue paint sparingly, working inwards from the points of the star. Wipe the back of the stencil to avoid smudging. Space the stars about 10 cm (4 in) apart along all the white stripes.*

9△ *Repeat with white paint on the red stripes, positioning the white stars to fall halfway between the blue stars.*

10◁ *Apply at least three coats of varnish. Use an antique tinted varnish if you wish to mellow the bright colours.*

Stamped Throw

✳ A casually draped throw is one of the essentials of country style, softening hard edges and hiding a multitude of sins. This floral design is adapted from an old appliqué quilt and has been translated into three stamps. Copy the colours shown here or adapt them to suit your own colour scheme. Special block-printing fabric ink in a wide range of colours is available from art and craft suppliers. Slightly textured fabric gives extra interest, but it should not be too irregular.

YOU WILL NEED

- **old blanket**
- **drawing pins (thumb tacks)**
- **three templates (see page 153)**
- **tracing paper and pencil (optional)**
- **spray mount adhesive**
- **1 cm (½ in) thick high-density foam**
- **craft knife and masking tape**
- **palette knife**
- **sheet of glass**
- **water-based block-printing fabric inks in two or more colours**
- **small gloss paint roller**
- **square of off-white cotton fabric, to the size required**
- **sewing machine and matching thread**

1 *Pin the blanket to a tabletop, using drawing pins, to allow some "give" when you stamp. Trace or photocopy the templates. Spray the back lightly with adhesive and stick on to three roughly cut pieces of foam.*

2 *Cut out the shapes with a craft knife, using sweeping hand movements rather than lots of small cuts. Use the craft knife to "draw" around each shape, then bend the foam to open the cut and pull away the excess foam.*

3 ◁ *Peel off the templates. Make a small handle out of masking tape for the back of each stamp.*

4 ▽ *Using a palette knife on a sheet of glass, mix two or more printing ink colours to give subtle tones.*

➤

5 *Run the paint roller through the ink and apply an even coating of colour to the straight border stamp.*

6 *Machine stitch a hem around all four edges of the fabric, then place it on the blanket. Position the stamp near one corner and apply even pressure. Lift off directly so as not to smudge the colour. Stamp squares all over the fabric.*

7 ◁ *Apply paint to the centre motif and place in the middle of a square, position-ing it by eye to give a natural, hand-printed look. Repeat with the other squares.*

8 ▽ *Wash the glass and paint roller, then change to the second ink colour. Add four leaf shapes to each square – don't worry if they overlap the border. Leave to dry.*

Appliqué Window quilt

The idea of a window quilt is practical as well as decorative. It is particularly good in the winter time as it keeps out draughts at night. The inspiration for this appliqué coffee cup design comes from an old American quilt pattern originally published in Chicago in the 1940s. The sentiment is hospitality, which makes it very welcoming in the kitchen. This quilt is hung very simply from curtain clips.

YOU WILL NEED

- two coffee cup templates (see page 154)
- tracing paper and pencil
- spray mount adhesive
- card (cardboard)
- craft knife
- cutting mat or large piece of thick card (cardboard)
- fine black felt-tipped pen
- 50 cm (½ yd) each of cotton fabric in mid-blue, red-brown and olive green
- scissors
- dressmaker's pins
- pre-washed natural calico, to fit the size of your window frame plus 5 cm (2 in) all round
- sewing needle and thread
- thin iron-on wadding (batting), the same size as the calico
- iron
- mid-blue cotton fabric, 7.5 cm (3 in) larger all around than the calico
- curtain clips

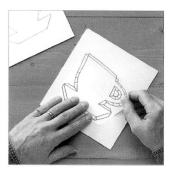

1 *Trace both coffee cup templates. Spray the back lightly with adhesive and stick on to card (cardboard).*

2 *Cut out the shapes, using a craft knife and a cutting mat or large piece of card (cardboard).*

3 *Using a felt-tipped pen, draw around the large cup shape on to each fabric colour. Draw about six cups at a time.*

4▷ *Place the smaller shape inside each outline. Draw the shape indicated by the fold lines and also the snip lines.*

➤

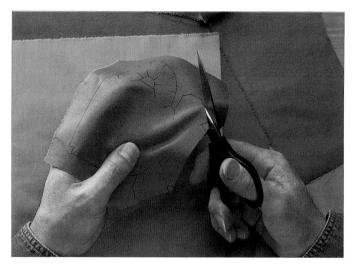

5 *Cut out the large coffee cup shapes.*

6▽ *Snip up to the fold line as marked on the curved edges.*

7◁ *Pin the coffee cups to the calico fabric, alternating the colours and spacing them evenly.*

8▷ *Using your thumbnail to crease the fabric, turn under a small hem around each shape.*

9◁ *Slip stitch around each shape, using the needle to tuck in untidy edges. Bring the needle up through the shape and directly down into the calico, then bring it up further along for the next stitch. Any irregularity is part of its charm.*

To make up the quilt:
Iron the wadding (batting) to the back of the calico, placing a cloth under the iron. Lay the blue backing fabric out flat and centre the quilt right side up on top. Fold the blue fabric over on all sides to make a border. Turn under the raw edges and slip stitch to the edge of the quilt. Attach curtain clips to the top.

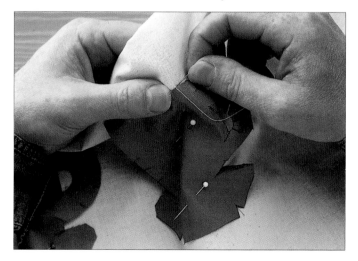

Rooster Cushion

✸ The handsome cockerel is a favourite motif in folk art all over the world. Its proud shape has been used to decorate everything from church spires to tin trays. This combination of gingham fabric and roosters is pure country style. The process used is photocopy transfer, which is done by photocopy shops that print T-shirts. The print is washable, but avoid direct contact with a hot iron.

YOU WILL NEED
- **rooster image (see page 153)**
- **scissors**
- **A3 (12in x 16in) sheet of white paper**
- **spray mount adhesive**
- **50 cm (½ yd) beige cotton fabric**
- **40 cm x 40 cm (16 in x 16 in) square of blue-and-beige gingham cotton fabric**
- **dressmaker's pins**
- **sewing machine and matching thread**
- **38 cm (15 in) square cushion pad**

1 *Photocopy the rooster image five times. Cut out the shapes roughly as shown.*

2 *Arrange the photocopies on the sheet of paper. Spray the back of each image with adhesive and stick in place.*

3 *Cut a 30 cm x 30 cm (12 in x 12 in) square of beige fabric and take it and the design to a photocopy shop. Ask them to make a transfer, which should also be trimmed to make a square. The transfer should be centred on the fabric square.*

4 *Turn under a small hem all around the printed fabric. Place on the right side of the gingham fabric, in the centre. Pin in place, then machine stitch.*

5 *Cut two beige cotton backing pieces 40 cm x 30 cm (16 in x 12 in). Stitch a hem on one long edge of each piece. Right sides together, place both pieces on the cushion front so that they align with the front at either side and overlap in the middle.*

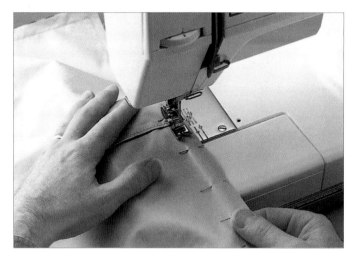

6 *Pin then stitch, adjusting the height of the needle if necessary to stitch through the four layers in the centre.*

7▷ *Clip across the corners. Turn the cushion cover right side out and insert the cushion pad.*

Cross stitch Napkin

★ Goodlooking cross stitch relies on the stitches being regular, so checked or gingham fabric makes an ideal ready-made grid. This very easy project is an ideal place to start if you have not done much embroidery before. The cotton fabric should be quite thick and coarsely woven, with a thick embroidery thread to match. Cross stitch will also add a handmade quality to a set of bought table napkins.

YOU WILL NEED

for four napkins

- **1 m (1 yd) heavyweight checked cotton fabric**
- **dressmaker's scissors**
- **dressmaker's pins**
- **needle and thread**
- **sewing machine and matching thread**
- **embroidery scissors**
- **stranded embroidery cotton (floss), in bright contrast colour**
- **embroidery needle**

1 *Cut the fabric into four rectangles 35 cm x 48 cm (14 in x 19 in). Turn under the raw edge on each side, then fold over again to make a narrow hem. Pin and tack (baste).*

2 *Machine stitch with matching thread, using straight or zigzag stitch.*

3 *Cut a length of embroidery thread double the width of the first napkin. Thread the embroidery needle, using all six strands, and knot the end. Leaving a blank row of checks, start at one end of a row of checks, with the knot on the reverse side. Make diagonal stitches across alternate squares to the end of the row. Finish with a neat double stitch.*

4 *Re-thread the needle as before, then work back along the same row, crossing over each diagonal stitch. Repeat to give a pattern of three cross stitch rows at both ends of each napkin.*

Squared Patchwork quilt

✳ This is the most basic of all patchwork patterns. It is quickly made on a sewing machine and really can be completed in a day! The fabrics used here have been chosen to give a restrained Shaker look. For a completely different result, use bright primary colours or a mix of small-patterned fabrics. Old country quilts often used recycled fabrics, so you could make a "memory" quilt out of your children's favourite outgrown clothes.

YOU WILL NEED

for a single bed-size quilt

- **1 m (1 yd) each of two different cotton fabrics**
- **tape measure**
- **dressmaker's scissors**
- **sewing machine and matching thread**
- **2 m (2 yd) medium-weight iron-on wadding (batting)**
- **iron**
- **brushed cotton single bed sheet**
- **50 cm (½ yd) contrast cotton fabric**
- **dressmaker's pins**
- **needle and matching thread**

1 *Cut an equal number of 19 cm (7½ in) squares in each fabric.*

2 *Machine stitch the squares together in rows, alternating the two fabrics. There should be nine squares in each row, starting alternate rows with the opposite colour. Make six rows altogether.*

3 *Stitch the rows together, aligning the squares.*

4 ▷ *Lay the wadding (batting) out flat with the patchwork right side up on top. Trim the wadding and reserve. Iron the patchwork, bonding the two together.*

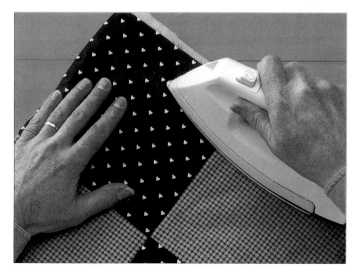

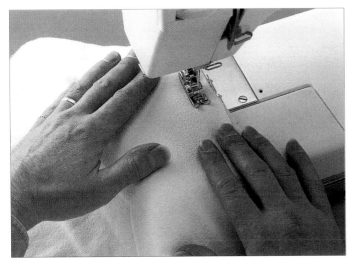

5 *Lay patchwork right side up on top of the sheet. Trim sheet to same size. Pin around the edge, then machine stitch.*

6 ▽ *Measure around the quilt, then cut enough 7.5 cm (3 in) wide strips of contrast fabric to make the edging.*

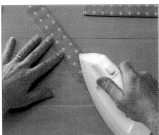

7 ◁ *Fold each strip in half, right side out. Iron the fold.*

8 ▷ *Cut strips of wadding (batting) 2.5 cm (1 in) wide. Push right inside the folded fabric strips, then iron both sides together.*

9 ◁ *Open out each strip and stitch to the front of the quilt as shown.*

10 ▽ *Fold the edging to the back of the quilt. Turn under a small hem and pin, enclosing all the raw edges.*

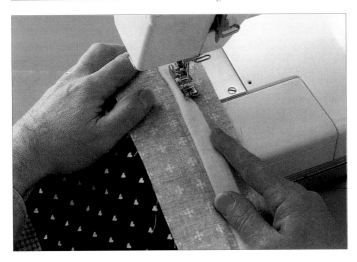

➤

11 *At the corners, enclose the side edging strips in the top and bottom edging strips.*

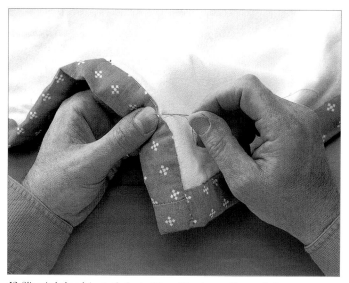

12 *Slip stitch the edging to the back of the quilt, using small neat stitches.*

Clover leaf Tablecloth

This fresh four-leaf clover pattern is done very simply with a potato print. The cut potato exudes a starchy liquid that blends into the ink and adds translucence. The best fabric to print on is 100% cotton, pre-washed to remove any glaze or stiffener. The result should look handprinted, so don't despair if the edge of the potato picks up colour and prints it occasionally – it will add energy and life to the pattern. If you take a short break, place the potato in iced water and dry with kitchen paper (paper towel).

YOU WILL NEED:

- **old blanket**
- **drawing pins (thumb tacks)**
- **medium-size fresh potato**
- **sharp knife and cutting board**
- **small artist's paintbrush**
- **craft knife**
- **sharp kitchen knife**
- **leaf green water-based block printing fabric ink (or standard primary colours: yellow, blue and red)**
- **sheet of glass**
- **palette knife**
- **small gloss paint roller**
- **white 100% cotton fabric, pre-washed and ironed, to fit your table**
- **sewing machine (optional) and matching thread**

1 *Pin the blanket to the tabletop, using drawing pins (thumb tacks) – this allows some "give" when you apply pressure. Cut through the potato in one smooth movement to give a flat surface.*

2 *Practise painting the clover leaf on paper, copying the pattern freehand. When you are confident, paint the shape on the potato.*

3 *Cut carefully around the shape, using a craft knife. Use smooth, flowing movements to avoid jagged edges. Cut around the internal shapes. Scoop out the potato flesh with the end of the knife blade.*

4 *Cut away the waste potato to a depth of about 6 mm (¼ in).*

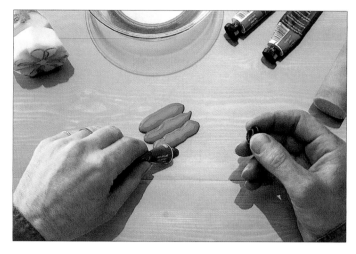

5 *Using a kitchen knife, trim the potato into a square. Cut a groove all around, about halfway down – this will make it easier to hold.*

6▷ *If you are using standard colours, mix 2 parts green, 1 part blue, ¼ red. Or use ready-mixed leaf green.*

7◁ *Blend the primary colours (if using) thoroughly on a sheet of glass, using a palette knife.*

8▷ *Run the paint roller through the ink until it is thoroughly coated.*

9 *Apply an even coating of ink to the potato stamp.*

10▷ *Lay the prepared fabric on the blanket and print the pattern at random. Re-ink the potato after every two printings to vary the intensity of the colour. Leave the finished fabric to dry, then hem the edges by hand or machine. Make matching napkins the same way.*

Hooked Rag rug

Rag rugs were originally a way of recycling old clothes to make soft, warm furnishings, but some of those that have survived are also works of art. The women who made them often used domestic objects such as dinner plates to make simple designs. You can trim the loops to give an even pile or leave the looped effect – both are traditional. You will get a better result if you use all wool fabrics, as they resist dirt and are comfortable underfoot. Tweed and blanket fabrics are ideal. It is a good idea to wash the fabrics first in hot water to felt the wool and give a firmer texture for cutting into strips.

YOU WILL NEED

- **coarse-weave hessian (burlap), to the finished size required plus 5 cm (2 in) all around**
- **fine black felt-tipped pen**
- **sewing needle and thread**
- **large-eyed darning needle and string**
- **wooden rugmaker's frame**
- **assortment of old woollen fabrics**
- **large scissors**
- **rug hook**

1 *Draw the outline of the rug size on the hessian (burlap), using a felt-tipped pen. Fold under a 5 cm (2 in) border all around and tack (baste).*

2 *Draw a simple design, either abstract or with stylized plants and animals.*

3 *Using string and the needle, wrap the hessian (burlap) around one end of the frame and secure with a running stitch. Repeat at other end. Assemble the frame.*

4◁ *Lace the sides of the hessian (burlap) to the frame, pulling it taut.*

5▽ *Cut the woollen fabrics as straight as possible into strips 6 mm–1 cm (¼ in–½ in) wide, depending on the strength of each fabric. Group the fabrics in colours.*

➤

6 *Fold the first strip of fabric in half. Hold between thumb and forefinger underneath the hessian (burlap) and hook to the surface with the other hand. (The photo shows the fabric underside.)*

7 *Pull up the strip to make a loop of about 1 cm (½ in).*

8 *Push the hook back down into the hessian (burlap) a few threads further along the design and repeat.*

9 *Spacing each loop depends on the width and thickness of the fabric strips, and it will come with practice.*

10 *Bring the ends of each strip to the surface and trim. Continue to hook the design, changing colour as necessary.*

11 *When complete, remove the rug from the frame. To bind the border, fold strips of plain fabric over the edge. Stitch in place, hiding the stitches in the ragwork.*

Accessories

In country style, accessories are useful rather than purely ornamental. This does not mean that they cannot be painted or decorated to look attractive, quite the contrary. Accessories are the finishing touch that makes all the difference between a room that has no individual character and one that feels part of a home. A collection of unusual and interesting objects does not arrive all at once but evolves over a period of time, and each treasure has its own story to tell. Visiting antique stalls, shops and fairs on a regular basis will soon reap results.

Right: The best country accessories usually look worn and loved, like this billy can, which looks perfect alongside the wire-work baskets and kitchen tools.

Country Accessories

Once you have transformed your home with country-style paint finishes, furniture, flooring and fabrics, it is time to add the finishing touches. The accumulation of "finds" that add personality to a home does take time, and it should be a gradual process: it often depends on your being in the right place at the right time. An unlimited supply of money would buy you folk-art treasures and an interior-designed country look, but you would certainly miss out on the pleasure of making your own accessories.

There are projects in this chapter to suit most talents and skills, whether your talent lies with a needle and thread, carpenter's tools or paintbrushes. We show how household objects such as buckets and laundry baskets can add pattern and colour as well as being useful for mundane practicalities. If you look at domestic folk art, everything was considered

worthy of decoration. In the narrowboats that carried coal and other heavy goods on the English canals, every jug, bowl and tray was richly ornamented with colourful paintwork. It is very satisfying to put to daily use something you have made or painted yourself.

Some of the projects require basic woodwork techniques. They can all be made on the kitchen table, but if you are not very experienced at woodwork you could perhaps find a friendly carpenter to cut the pieces for you to assemble and paint. A local carpenter may also use reclaimed

Above: A fresh coat of white paint and stencilled strawberries have been used here to give a dull window box a country garden look.

Left: A rescued crate stencilled with grapevines and lined with straw makes a perfect nesting place for a collection of wine.

timber such as old pine floorboards. It is really worth using for its character and colour. An ideal woodwork project to start with is the Framed Chalkboard. After this, try The Knife Box. It is a very traditional kitchen accessory, painted to look authentically old.

Baskets, bottles and china can all be given the country treatment, often very simply indeed. Don't be too precise about matching accessories to your existing furnishings – in this style of decorating, individual touches and character are far more important than co-ordination.

Above: *Stunning but simple, this cross stitch patterned peg bag will brighten up your washing line and relieve the wash-day blues.*

Right: *The tradition of painting household objects such as this watering can goes back a long way. Use muted colours and traditional patterns to create folk art of your own.*

Stencilled Bucket

✳ Turn an ordinary bucket into a stylish garden accessory with two cans of spray paint and a simple stencil. This pretty decoration is based on an old design discovered on the original stencilled walls in a Rhode Island house. Spray paint dries very quickly if you use it sparingly. Repeat the flower design four times around the side of the bucket.

YOU WILL NEED
- **flower and border templates (see page 154)**
- **tracing paper and pencil (optional)**
- **spray mount adhesive**
- **stencil card (cardboard)**
- **craft knife**
- **cutting mat or thick card (cardboard)**
- **spray paint in bright green and yellow**
- **galvanized or enamel bucket**
- **masking tape**
- **scrap paper**

1 *Trace or photocopy the templates. Spray the back lightly with adhesive and stick them on to stencil card (cardboard). Carefully cut out the shapes, using a craft knife and cutting mat or thick card (cardboard). Peel off the paper templates.*

2 *In a well-ventilated area, spray the bucket with green spray paint. Leave to dry thoroughly.*

3 *Spray the back of the flower stencil lightly with adhesive. Position the stencil on the side of the bucket.*

4 *Using masking tape, attach scrap paper around the stencil. Spray the stencil lightly with yellow paint. Lift off carefully when dry to the touch and re-position. Spray the borders in the same way.*

Framed Chalkboard

✸ Once you have had a chalkboard in the kitchen it becomes one of life's absolute essentials, far more satisfying to use than any other form of memo pad. The frame is made of an old plank sawn into four pieces – two long, two short – which are simply glued together. Choose the size to suit your wall space. Cramp the frame while the glue sets or hold it together with string, twisting a pencil in the string to tighten it.

YOU WILL NEED

- stencil templates (see page 155)
- tracing paper and pencil (optional)
- spray mount adhesive
- stencil card (cardboard)
- craft knife and cutting mat
- emulsion (latex) paint: dull blue and red
- small decorator's paintbrush
- old white plate
- medium-grade sandpaper
- stencil brush
- artist's acrylic paint in black
- antiquing varnish and brush
- hardboard, 2.5 cm (1 in) larger all around than the inner frame measurement
- blackboard paint
- hammer and panel pins (small fine nails)
- (you will also need a piece of chalk!)

1 *Trace or photocopy the templates, enlarging them if necessary. Spray the back lightly with adhesive and stick on to stencil card (cardboard). Cut out the shapes, using a craft knife and cutting mat.*

2 *Paint the frame with blue emulsion (latex). Leave to dry.*

3 *Paint the inner and outer edges of the frame with red emulsion (latex). Leave to dry.*

4▽ *Rub the paint with sandpaper to reveal the grain of the wood.*

➤

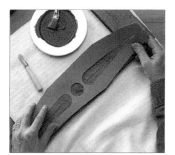

5 *Spray the back of each stencil lightly and position on the frame. Arrange the shapes as shown in the main picture.*

6 *Using a stencil brush, apply the red paint.*

7 *Darken the red paint by mixing in a little black acrylic paint.*

8◁ *Using the stencil brush, rub the dark red paint deep into the grain in just a few places.*

9▽ *When dry, rub over with sandpaper to remove any dark red paint from the surface.*

10 *Apply a coat of antiquing varnish. Leave to dry.*

11 *Paint the hardboard with two coats of blackboard paint. Leave to dry.*

12 *Fix the blackboard to the back of the frame, using panel pins (small fine nails).*

Decorated Lampshade

Customize a plain shop-bought lampshade with this pretty country-style decoration. Use long lengths of embroidery thread for the borders so that there will be no loose ends to show through when the lamp is lit. An alternative colour scheme would be natural linen-look fabric combined with coffee-coloured ribbons and pearl or wooden buttons.

YOU WILL NEED

- **neutral-coloured plain fabric lampshade**
- **dressmaker's pins**
- **embroidery scissors**
- **red stranded embroidery cotton (floss) – separate the strands and use three in the needle**
- **embroidery needle**
- **two heart templates (see page 155)**
- **tracing paper and pencil**
- **remnant of red-and-white gingham fabric**
- **scissors**
- **iron-on fabric stiffener**
- **iron**
- **scraps of red-and-white gingham ribbon or bias binding**
- **small white and brown buttons**
- **fabric glue**

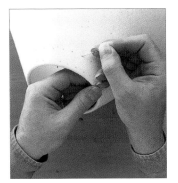

1 *Using a pin, pierce tiny holes around the top and bottom of the lampshade as a grid for the cross stitches.*

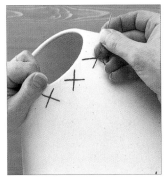

2 *Cut a long length of embroidery cotton (floss) and knot the end. Starting inside the lampshade, work single cross stitches around the top. Use two long lengths of thread around the bottom – work diagonal stitches close together in one direction then use a second thread to cross back in the opposite direction.*

3 *Trace the two heart templates. Cut out three hearts from the gingham fabric, using the large template.*

4 *Using the small template, cut three hearts from fabric stiffener. Centre on the back of the gingham hearts and iron. Make small squares and diamonds in the same way.*

5 *Work a line of running stitch around the edge of the fabric stiffener on each shape. Pull out the threads outside this line to make a fringe.*

6 *Cut two short equal lengths of ribbon or bias binding. Stitch together with a button to make a cross. Repeat as needed to decorate your lampshade.*

7 *Arrange the gingham and ribbon shapes, then secure with fabric glue.*

8 *Fill in any gaps with single cross stitches.*

Rustic Knife box

The inspiration for this rustic knife box comes from Ireland, where they were traditionally a feature in every rural kitchen. The stepped design means that knives of different lengths can be stored safely. The unusual paint finish could be used on any other piece of painted wooden furniture or accessory in the book to give an instant aged look.

YOU WILL NEED
- knife box
- acrylic paint: dull red and burnt umber
- old white plate
- small decorator's paintbrush
- rubber gloves
- small piece of natural sponge
- paint stripper
- old cloths
- antiquing wax
- soft polishing cloth

1 *Paint the knife box very roughly with red paint, using random strokes and leaving plenty of gaps. Leave to dry.*

2 *Paint on the burnt umber paint in the same way. Leave until completely dry.*

3 *Wearing rubber gloves, sponge on a dappled coat of paint stripper so that the paint is lifted in some places only.*

4 *Immediately wipe over with a wet cloth to neutralize the effect and wash away blistered fragments of paint.*

5 *When dry, rub in a generous coat of antiquing wax. Then buff the wax with a soft cloth to give a rich sheen.*

Simple Spongeware

Sponging looks as good on china as it does on your walls. Commercial spongeware is fired in a kiln, but you can create the same effect at home using acrylic enamel paint. This is for decorative rather than food use, so stop the sponging short of the rim if you want to use the jug (pitcher) for drinking. The little cat stencil is applied first then masked off with a medallion shape so that it stands out against the green sponging.

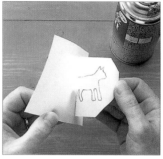

1 *Trace the cat template. Spray the back lightly with adhesive and stick on to stencil plastic or card (cardboard).*

2 *Using a craft knife with a sharp blade, cut out the cat shape, moving the stencil to cut smooth curves.*

YOU WILL NEED
- **medallion and cat templates (see page 152, 155)**
- **tracing paper and pencil**
- **stencil plastic or card (cardboard)**
- **craft knife**
- **cutting mat or thick card (cardboard)**
- **scissors**
- **spray mount adhesive**
- **plain white glazed china jug (pitcher)**
- **acrylic enamel paint: brown, yellow-orange, yellow and blue**
- **old white plate**
- **small piece of natural sponge**

3 *Trace the medallion template and cut out the paper shape. Spray the back of the cat stencil lightly with adhesive.*

➤

4 *Position the stencil on the jug (pitcher) and stick in place.*

5 *Add a small amount of brown to the yellow-orange enamel paint to make a deep orange colour.*

6 *Using a small sponge, sponge the deep orange paint on to the stencil.*

7 *Leave to dry then peel off the stencil.*

8 *Mix the yellow and blue paint to get a deep green colour.*

9 *Spray the back of the medallion shape with adhesive. Centre over the cat and stick in place.*

10 *Sponge the deep green paint evenly over the whole jug (pitcher). If you want to use it for drinks, stop 2.5 cm (1 in) short of the rim; otherwise apply the paint more densely around the rim and the medallion.*

11▷ *Peel off the paper medallion. Bake the jug (pitcher) in the oven for about 45 minutes, following the manufacturer's instructions.*

Painted Tin frame

✳ Pierced and painted tin is very popular in countries where materials are scarce and everything is recycled. This project is inspired by vibrantly painted Mexican tinware but the material used here is heavyweight aluminium foil, which can be bought from art and craft suppliers. It can be cut with scissors and bent to shape very easily, and it is not as dangerous as working with tin cans. Any blunt-ended instrument can be used to inscribe the patterns. Here this is done with the plastic-coated end of a paintbrush.

YOU WILL NEED
- **heavyweight aluminium foil**
- **large scissors**
- **broad, flat wooden frame**
- **paintbrush or other blunt-ended instrument**
- **drinking glass**
- **hammer**
- **broad-headed tacks**
- **nail varnish (polish): shocking pink and blue**

1 *Cut strips of foil to fit the sides of the frame. Fold the foil around the frame.*

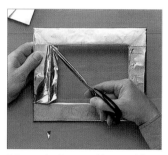

2 *Repeat for the top and bottom of the frame, mitring the corners to give a neat finish.*

3◁ *Using the end of a paintbrush, press a repeat wave pattern into the foil all around the frame.*

4▽*Cut pieces of foil slightly larger than the drinking glass.*

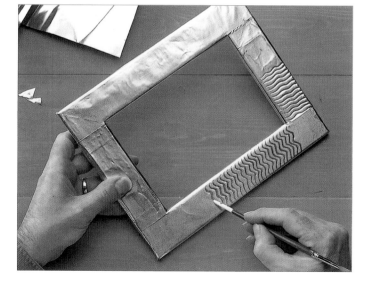

5 *Mark a semi-circle around the glass on to each piece of foil. Remove the glass, then square off the shape.*

6 *Cut out the semi-circles, adding scallops on the curved edges.*

7 *Cut out four fanned leaf shapes, also with scalloped edges.*

8 ◁ *Inscribe patterns on all the shapes as shown.*

9 ▽ *Arrange the shapes around the frame, with the undecorated straight edges at the back of the frame. Attach to the frame with tacks, then fold into place at the front.*

10 ◁ *Paint some details of the decorative border with pink nail varnish (polish).*

11 ▷ *Paint some extra details and the inner edge of the frame with blue nail varnish (polish).*

Painted Glass bottle

✹ This design is based on the famous Steigel glassware from 18th-century America, using simple folk art motifs of hearts and flowers. When you paint on glass, nothing can be concealed. This does not mean that you need to be meticulous – on the contrary, the painting should be full of life and vitality. Before you begin, shake your hand and wrist to get rid of any tension, then enjoy the way the paint flows on to the smooth glass surface.

YOU WILL NEED
- **interesting-shaped bottle (the irregularities of recycled glass suit this style very well)**
- **acrylic enamel paint in yellow, blue, red and white**
- **old white plate**
- **no. 3 and no. 5 watercolour brushes**
- **no. 1 lining brush**

1 *Wash the bottle in detergent and hot water. Dry thoroughly.*

2 *Mix yellow and blue paint to give a leaf green. Using each brush in turn, practise single stokes on the plate, varying the pressure to see the effect.*

3 *Lay the bottle on a flat surface. Paint the stems and leaves freehand, supporting your painting hand with your other hand.*

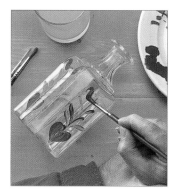

4 *Add flowers and hearts in red paint, using the direction of the brushstroke to describe the shape. Leave to dry for about 15 minutes.*

5 *Mix some white paint into the leaf green to make a much paler shade. Decorate the red flowers and hearts with rows of tiny dots.*

Painted Laundry basket

✴ Help take the drudgery out of washing and ironing with this painted wicker basket, decorated with random splashes of colour. Two different colour schemes are shown here, or you can choose your own. The same treatment could be used to smarten up an old Lloyd loom chair or table.

YOU WILL NEED
- **wicker laundry basket**
- **emulsion (latex) paint in base colour**
- **large decorator's paintbrush**
- **small pots of emulsion (latex) or acrylic paint in three bright contrasting colours**
- **stiff-bristled artist's paintbrush (for oil painting)**

1 *Paint the basket inside and out with the base colour. Apply the paint sparingly, otherwise it will build up in the weave and take a long time to dry.*

2 *When dry, add a few splashes of the first contrast colour with the artist's paintbrush.*

3 ▷ *Add splashes of the other colours, washing the brush between each colour. Leave to dry.*

Details

I t is often the final details that count in a decorating scheme, so here we concentrate on small things that make a big difference.

A love affair with the country style can be sparked off by a humble piece of wirework as much as by an elaborate piece of painted furniture. It is the small things, like using twine instead of string to tie up a bunch of fresh bay leaves or little wrought iron hooks along a shelf edge in place of plastic ones, that make all the difference.

Right: *Clay pots and wooden garden sieves are a pleasure to work with, and what better container could you find for cut flowers than a traditional garden trug? Carry your country style outdoors and enjoy the sensual pleasure of filling cool ter-racotta pots with compost on an old wooden potting bench.*

Country Details

Above: *A wonderful natural display can be made out of drying flowers by using simple garden twine between a pair of hooks.*

Left: *The neutral colours of glazed earthenware jars, marble surfaces and glass are a cool combination alongside the rich deep blue trim of this beautiful antique plate. The matching blue beads and handles reinforce the theme.*

As you add details, little by little, you will add your own personality and style to your home. For example, if you combine fabrics such as gingham with stripes, checks or tiny floral prints, you will gradually create a riot of colour and pattern that will appear as interesting tones in a larger scheme. Aim for an eclectic mix of colour, pattern and fabric. Use the ideas suggested in this chapter as a starting point, adding your own colour schemes and patterns to give each thing you make a personal touch.

There are many country crafts that can be studied and mastered, like weaving or the carving of decoy birds. If you have the time to explore and learn how things are traditionally made, it is very enriching. The pro-

jects in this chapter are more about taking short cuts and making an impact, which is a good creative starting point. Once you realize the pleasure that is to be gained from both making and displaying your own creations, you are bound to continue to experiment and to enjoy country crafts. You can add initials and dates to make a gift or family keepsake even more personal.

The Rolling Pin Holder and the Beaded Jug Cover are made from basic materials such as wire and net (tulle), perfect in a country kitchen. Traditions need to be constantly updated, and the modern version of the beaded cover would not look at all out of place at a summer barbecue, keeping away the wasps. The Tree of Life Picture is an ideal project for a

rainy day, a way to unwind by doodling with a set of watercolour paints. This and the set of Framed Memories pictures are very personal mementoes, things you could never buy in a shop.

Indoor wreaths made of herbs and spices are the essence of country style. Two very different ones are shown here, an elegant Bay Wreath and a Cornucopia Wreath, both extending a traditional country welcome to your home. Nature offers so many exquisite textures and colours. Scour the countryside, dried-flower stockist and even your own store cupboard for flowers, leaves, grasses and dried whole spices: collect richly textured strings, raffias and twines, and then transform them into lasting natural treasures.

These finishing touches are all very easy to make and are wonderful either for your own home or as gifts.

Above: *Never miss an opportunity to show off your treasures. Here a wirework wall hanging is used to display two very different hearts and a plain enamel mug.*

Right: *Mr and Mrs Gingerbread make wonderful old-fashioned cookies and, when not in use, they can be hung from a nail on the wall.*

Découpage Door knobs

⁕ Rejuvenate a chest-of-drawers with a fresh coat of dark green paint, then decorate the knobs with brightly coloured flowers. The same idea would look good on a single door knob. Gloss varnish gives the knobs an enamelled look, different from the usual country style but very effective here. The more coats of varnish you apply, the better the effect.

YOU WILL NEED
- **round wooden knobs**
- **artist's acrylic paint in yellow and red**
- **small paintbrush**
- **poppy template (see page 155)**
- **small, sharp pair of pointed scissors**
- **PVA (white) glue and brush**
- **clear gloss varnish and brush**
- **fine sandpaper**

1 *Paint the knobs yellow. Leave to dry then apply a second coat.*

2 *Photocopy the poppy template, making one copy for each knob. Dilute the red paint with water and paint the poppies. Leave to dry.*

3 *Cut out the poppies. Move the paper towards the scissors as you cut, and work slowly to avoid cutting angles instead of curves.*

4 *Coat the back of each poppy with glue, right up to the edges. Stick a poppy on to the centre of each knob.*

5 *Apply several coats of clear gloss varnish. Allow each coat to dry thoroughly, then rub lightly with sandpaper between coats.*

Rolling pin Holder

✳ This clever little device will give your rolling pin a place of its own on the kitchen wall, decorative as well as out of the way. Instead of purchasing a roll of wire, you can recycle two wire coathangers. Practise bending the wire before you start to master making smooth curves rather than sharp angles.

YOU WILL NEED
• **roll of 2 mm (⅒ in) wire**
• **wire-cutters and pliers (combined)**
• **screwdriver**
• **fine brass picture-hanging wire**

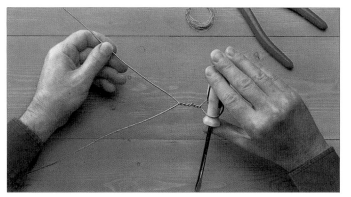

1 *Cut two lengths of wire 75 cm (30 in) each. Take one length, find the middle and bend it around a screwdriver to make a loop. Turn the screwdriver to twist the two halves of wire together six times.*

2 *Using the pliers, curl the two ends of the wire forwards.*

3▽ *Twist the second length of wire into a heart shape – bend it sharply in the middle, then bring the ends down in opposite directions so that they cross over. Curl the ends.*

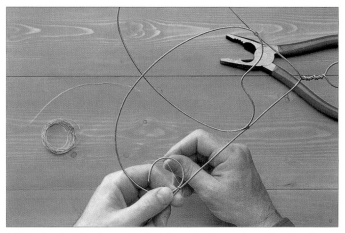

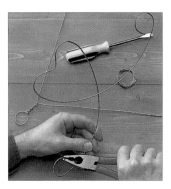

4 *Using short lengths of brass wire, bind the two lengths together at the points shown. Place your rolling pin between the curled hooks to judge the width needed.*

Framed Memories

Buy readymade box frames and give them the country treatment with a simple paint finish. Fill each frame with a miniature collection based on a particular holiday or theme – autumn leaves, pressed flowers or a seaside collection of pebbles, shells and driftwood. Mix textures and shapes, perhaps including an entrance ticket from a day out.

YOU WILL NEED

- **set of deep, square box frames**
- **masking tape**
- **acrylic paint: sky blue, brick red and dark green**
- **small decorator's paintbrush**
- **fine-grade sandpaper**
- **shellac and brush**
- **collection of natural objects**
- **glue gun and sticks**

1 *Stick masking tape around the edge of the glass of each frame to protect it from the paint. Paint the frame, choosing a colour to suit your collection.*

2 *When dry, rub with sandpaper to reveal the grain.*

3 *Apply a coat of shellac to mellow the colour of the paint. When dry, peel off the masking tape.*

4 *Paint the backing card (cardboard) with shellac.*

5 *Arrange the design on the backing card (cardboard), then glue in place. Leave to dry, then assemble the frame.*

Beaded Jug cover

✳ This is a simplified and modernized version of the intricate crochet and beadwork covers that were once a feature of every country pantry. Stitching through a paper pattern works very well because the stitches perforate the paper, making it very easy to tear off later. You can use a sewing machine, if you prefer.

YOU WILL NEED
- jug cover template (see page 157)
- ruler and pencil
- thin paper
- scissors
- 25 cm (¼ yd) white net (tulle)
- dressmaker's pins
- needle and matching thread
- 50 cm (½ yd) gingham bias binding
- sewing machine (optional)
- eight heavy beads, in bright colours

1 *Trace the jug cover template on to the thick paper and cut out. Repeat with the thin paper.*

2 *Fold the net to make a double layer. Pin the paper pattern to the net with a single pin. Stitch around the edge of the paper. Cut away the excess net.*

3 *Stitch one edge of the bias binding around the octagon, with the paper still in place. Pull away the paper pattern.*

4 *Fold the bias binding over to the other side of the net and stitch around the edge.*

5 *Space the beads evenly around the cover. Stitch to the bias binding, using a double loop of thread. Leave about 2.5 cm (1 in) drop of thread between each bead and the binding, then twist the end of the thread around this several times before fastening it off in the binding.*

Bay Wreath

✳ Bunches of herbs hang in every self-respecting country kitchen, but this lovely wreath makes them into a decorative feature. The frame of the wreath is simply made from a recycled wire coathanger, which of course makes it very easy to hang up. Green tape and gardening string are both available from florists or garden centres.

YOU WILL NEED
- wire coathanger
- green tape
- gardening string
- scissors
- sprigs of bay leaves
- wide green gingham ribbon

1 *Pull the coathanger into a circle with your hands, leaving the hanging hook as it is.*

2 *Bind the hook with green tape.*

3◁ *Using gardening string, tie sprigs of bay leaves on to the wire frame. Gradually build up a regular bushy shape.*

4▽ *Cut five lengths of ribbon and tie on to the wreath in simple bows.*

Cornucopia Wreath

✳ This style of wreath started in Scandinavia as a Christmas decoration, hung on the front door to welcome guests. Any mixture of nuts, herbs and spices can be used. For the base, use cuttings from a vine or similar plant, such as honeysuckle. Or ready-made natural wreath bases are available from some florists.

YOU WILL NEED
- vine cuttings or ready-made natural wreath base
- gardening string
- pliers
- gardening wire
- PVA (white) glue and brush
- old plate
- walnuts
- offcuts (scraps) of plaid or gingham fabric
- dried chillies
- small wicker baskets
- bay leaves
- dried apple rings
- cinnamon sticks

1 *Bend some of the longer cuttings into a circle and tie securely with string.*

2 *Weave more cuttings around the circle to make a solid base.*

3 *Cut short lengths of wire, dip in glue, then poke the ends into the walnut shells. Leave to dry.*

4 *Tear the fabric into strips. The frayed edges will give a homespun look.*

5 *Tie bunches of chillies together with string (don't rub your eyes!), then tie a fabric bow above each bunch. Twist several walnut wires together to make bunches, adding more bows. Pack the baskets with bay leaves and tie string on to the handles.*

6 *Tie all these objects on to the wreath. Fill the gaps with bunches of apple rings and cinnamon sticks, also tied with string.*

7 *Tie a loop of fabric at the top of the wreath for hanging.*

Decoy Birds

✻ Originally wooden birds were made for the practical purpose of deceiving real birds to fly down before the hunter's gun. Today decoy birds are very collectable and also very expensive, so it is well worth making your own. These colourful little birds are sawn from an old plank. The rustic effect is enhanced by using a piece of rough weathered wood for the base.

YOU WILL NEED
• bird templates (see page 156)
• tracing paper and pencil
• thin card (cardboard)
• scissors
• fine black felt-tipped pen
• floorboard or other piece of reclaimed timber
• clamp
• bradawl (awl)
• keyhole saw
• hand drill and 7 mm (⅜ in) bit
• 1 m (38 in) of 7 mm (⅜ in) dowelling
• small hacksaw
• piece of driftwood or rough weathered wood
• artist's acrylic paints: red, yellow, dark green, dark brown, white and black
• small decorator's paintbrush
• old white plate
• medium artist's paintbrush
• fine-grade sandpaper
• PVA (white) glue
• clear matt (flat) varnish and brush (optional)

3▷ *Clamp the board to a solid surface. With a bradawl (awl), make a hole at the edge of the first shape. Insert the blade of a keyhole saw through the hole and saw around the marked line. Repeat for the other birds.*

1 *Trace the templates and transfer on to thin card (cardboard). Cut out with scissors.*

2 *Using a felt-tipped pen, draw around each bird shape on to the floorboard or piece of reclaimed timber.*

➤

4 *Drill a hole in the bottom centre of each bird.*

5 *Cut the dowelling into five pieces, three 20 cm (8 in) long and two 18 cm (7 in) long.*

6 *Drill five holes in the piece of driftwood or rough wood, spacing them far enough apart for the birds to sit comfortably.*

7 *Paint the birds, each in a different colour. Leave to dry.*

8 *Add beaks and eyes in black paint. Leave to dry.*

9 *Rub over the paint with sandpaper to reveal the wood along the edges of each bird.*

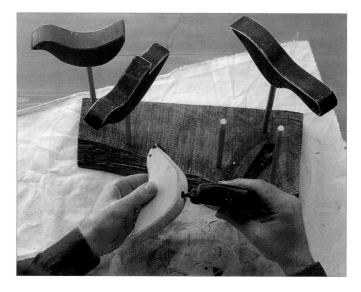

10 ◁ *Glue the pieces of dowelling into the holes in the base. Glue the birds on top to make an attractive group. If desired, apply a coat of varnish.*

Collage Tree of Life

✹ The Tree of Life is a favourite subject for folk artists working in many different media. Here we have used a collage of watercolour scraps to make a very individual framed picture. Templates are supplied for the main shapes, but the essential character of the picture lies in its handmade, naive quality. Cut the shapes freehand, rather than tracing them, to achieve a dynamic, spontaneous look.

You will need

- **large sheet of watercolour paper**
- **scissors**
- **set of watercolour paints**
- **selection of watercolour brushes**
- **white china mixing palette or old white plate**
- **small piece of natural sponge**
- **large sheet of handmade paper**
- **picture frame**
- **design shapes (see page 157)**
- **fine black felt-tipped pen**
- **PVA (white) glue and brush *or* spray mount adhesive**

1 *Cut the watercolour paper into small pieces. Using watercolour paints, spend at least an hour painting different patterns.*

2 *Use a sponge to add a different texture to some of the patterns.*

3 *Cut the handmade paper to fit the frame.*

4▷ *Paint a piece of watercolour paper plain green and fold in half. Using a felt-tipped pen, draw branch shapes, leaving a narrow space on the fold for the tree trunk. Follow the design shapes for reference. Cut out the branches, then open out the tree shape.*

5 *Cut different flower shapes from your patterned papers.*

6 *Cut leaves, berries and birds the same way. Cut a base for the tree to sit on.*

7 *Glue the tree trunk and branches in the centre of the handmade paper.*

8 *Add the main flowers and the base of the tree.*

9 *Build up your own Tree of Life, adding all the other elements. Finally, add the birds. Fit the collage into the frame.*

Basic Equipment

The most important equipment in country decorating is a good selection of paintbrushes to help you achieve the paint effects shown in the projects.

Graining brush This wide brush is used to drag off a freshly painted glaze. Apply it in a straight line to give a striped effect, or wiggle it occasionally to imitate wood grain.

4 cm (1½ in) watercolour brush A soft brush made of manmade fibres, this has many of the qualities of fine sable brushes. It is good for applying thinned colour.

Medium (4 cm/1½ in) decorator's paintbrush.

Claw hammer Used to insert and remove nails.

Fine-grade sandpaper This is needed in many projects to finish and smooth wood surfaces.

Medium-grade sandpaper This coarser texture is used to rub back paint to reveal the grain underneath.

Ink roller This rubber roller is used to apply ink evenly on to a printing block or stamp.

Wire-cutters These very strong and sharp steel cutters are needed for wirework.

Natural sponge A decorator's sponge is much cheaper than a bathroom sponge.

Staple gun This is a multi-purpose tool, especially useful in upholstery.

Gloss paint roller This small foam roller is sold for use with gloss paint but can also be used for other purposes such as striping walls.

No. 2 lining brush A long-haired fine watercolour brush, used for painting lines.

No. 5 watercolour brush This is a medium-sized soft brush. Vary the pressure to give lines of different width.

Scissors It is worth having a good sharp pair.

Key to picture

1 Graining brush
2 Watercolour brush
3 Medium decorator's paintbrush
4 Claw hammer
5 Fine-grade sandpaper
6 Medium-grade sandpaper
7 Ink roller
8 Wire-cutters
9 Natural sponge
10 Staple gun
11 Gloss paint roller
12 No. 2 lining brush
13 No. 5 watercolour brush
14 Scissors

Basic Materials

Country style requires very few specialist materials – the simpler, the better. These are some of the more unusual materials used in the various projects.

Wood stain A liquid stain applied to bare wood. The stain is absorbed into the wood so the grain shows through.

White wood stain This is applied to bare wood to give a limed effect.

Artist's acrylic paints Available in tubes, the colours can be mixed together and thinned with water. The paints can be used on most surfaces, and also to tint emulsion (latex) paint. Strengthen the finish by applying a coat of varnish.

Heavy-gauge foil Sold by craft suppliers, this can be cut with scissors and inscribed with any blunt instrument. Copper, brass and aluminium foil are available.

High-density foam Used to make stamps, this is available at specialist foam suppliers. You can also use compact sleeping mats from camping suppliers.

Chicken wire This is available from garden centres and hardware stores in different widths and with holes of various sizes.

Antiquing wax This tinted beeswax polish is used to subtly age new wood.

Japan gold size This is a type of glue that is painted on to the surface and left until tacky before applying sheets of gold leaf.

Acrylic enamel paint This multipurpose, opaque, water-based paint can be painted on to glass or china, then baked in a domestic oven to fix the design permanently.

Stranded embroidery cotton This comes in six strands, which can be separated. Use as many strands as you wish, depending on the thickness of thread required. A wide range of colours is available.

Block-printing ink This water-based ink is specially designed for printing on to fabric.

Linen tea towel This is a very useful fine-woven fabric, sometimes printed with checks or stripes at either end.

Unbleached cotton A natural country fabric, ideal for printed or stamped designs.

Weathered wood Use reclaimed timber whenever possible.

Key to picture

1 Wood stain

2 White wood stain

3 Artist's acrylic paints

4 Heavy-gauge foil

5 High-density foam

6 Chicken wire

7 Antiquing wax

8 Japan gold size

9 Acrylic enamel paint

10 Stranded embroidery cotton

11 Block-printing ink

12 Linen tea towel

13 Unbleached cotton

14 Weathered wood

Basic Techniques

✳ Many of these techniques are used in more than one project, and you can often combine techniques very effectively. Once you have mastered a few simple skills, you will be able to tackle projects of some complexity with confidence.

Painting
Most of the paint used in this book is matt emulsion (flat latex) applied directly on to the surface, without a priming coat of paint underneath. This is a very typical country finish. The paintwork can be strengthened with a coat of matt (flat) varnish.

1 Paint directly on to the bare wood. Leave to dry.

2 Rub the surface with fine-grade wire wool (steel wool) to remove some of the paint and give a naturally worn effect.

3 Fine-grade sandpaper is more abrasive than wire wool (steel wool). The paint will only remain visible in the recesses of the wood grain.

Antiquing wax
This tinted beeswax can be worked into the surface, grain and corners of wood to give the effect of subtle ageing. It is very good for the wood and will fill your room with the sweet smell of beeswax.

1 Using a soft, clean cloth, rub the wax into the wood. Use it sparingly, applying more if needed.

2 Work the wax into all the grooves, grain and corners, using an old toothbrush.

3 Finally polish the surface to a soft sheen with a soft cloth. As you rub, you warm the wax, which becomes aromatic.

Stencilling

This old-fashioned technique is really just a cut-out shape in a piece of card (cardboard). You can buy ready-made stencils in many country designs, but it is far more satisfying to make your own.

1 *Draw your own design on to paper, or alternatively trace or photocopy one of the templates supplied. Spray the back lightly with spray mount adhesive and stick on to stencil card (cardboard).*

2 *The best way to cut out a stencil is to hold the craft knife at a slight angle. Cut from the outer points of the shape in towards the centre. You will also find it easier if you re-position the card (cardboard) as you work, rather than the craft knife.*

3 *Peel off the paper pattern. Spray the back of the stencil lightly with spray mount adhesive and position it on the surface you wish to stencil.*

Masking

Masking tape is very useful if you need to paint a straight line or stripe. It also keeps the paint off part of a design when you are applying an all-over treatment such as spray paint or sponging.

1 *To paint a line, attach two parallel lines of masking tape on to the surface, leaving a narrow gap in between. Paint down the line – it does not matter if the paint overlaps the tape as the masking tape protects the surface.*

2 *When the paint is dry, peel off the masking tape.*

3 *To mask off an area, cut out a piece of paper to the required shape. Spray lightly with spray mount adhesive and stick it in place. Paint the surface and then leave to dry. Once dry, remove the paper.*

Templates

Bronze chair
page 48
75%

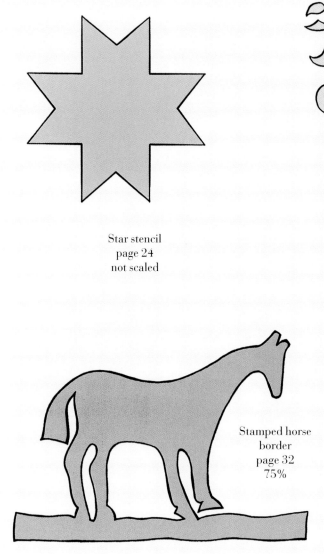

Star stencil
page 24
not scaled

Stamped horse
border
page 32
75%

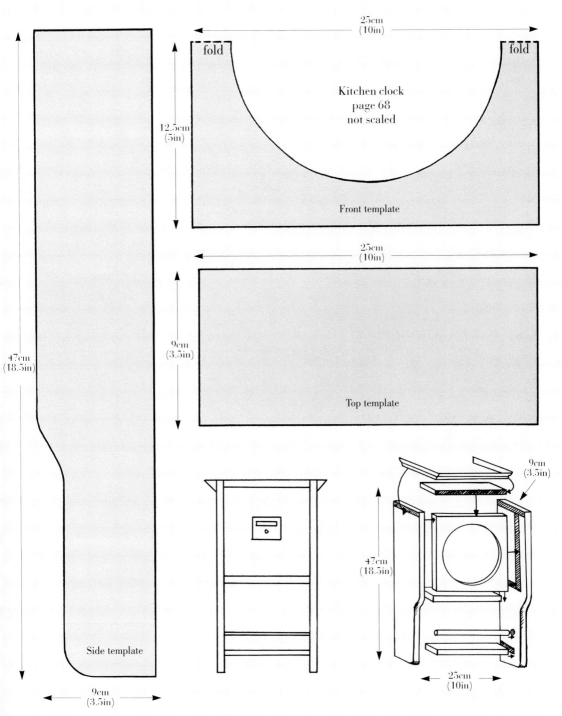

25cm
(10in)

fold   fold

Kitchen clock
page 68
not scaled

12.5cm
(5in)

Front template

25cm
(10in)

9cm
(3.5in)

Top template

47cm
(18.5in)

Side template

9cm
(3.5in)

9cm
(3.5in)

47cm
(18.5in)

25cm
(10in)

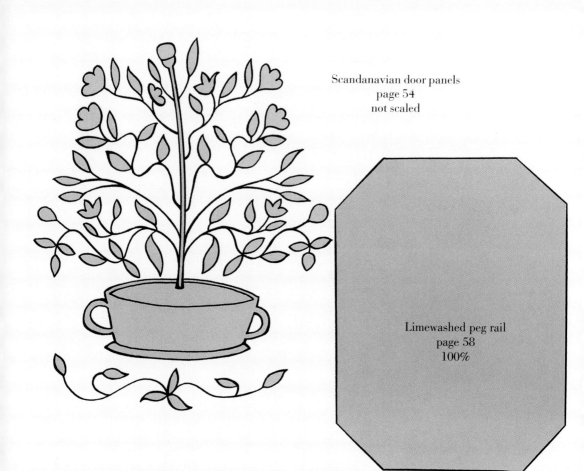

Scandanavian door panels
page 54
not scaled

Limewashed peg rail
page 58
100%

123

Rooster cushion
page 83
100%

Stamped throw
page 77
100%

Stars and stripes
floor cloth
page 74
100%

Appliqué
window quilt
page 80
100%

Stencilled bucket
page 102
100%

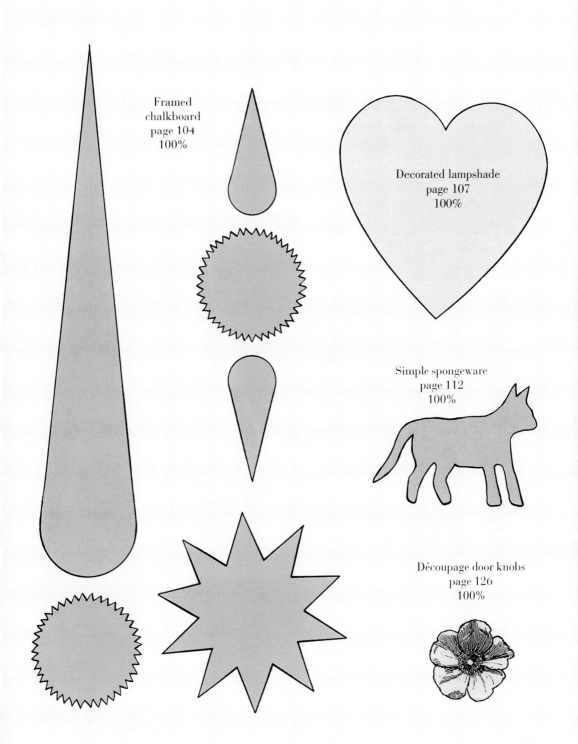

Framed
chalkboard
page 104
100%

Decorated lampshade
page 107
100%

Simple spongeware
page 112
100%

Découpage door knobs
page 126
100%

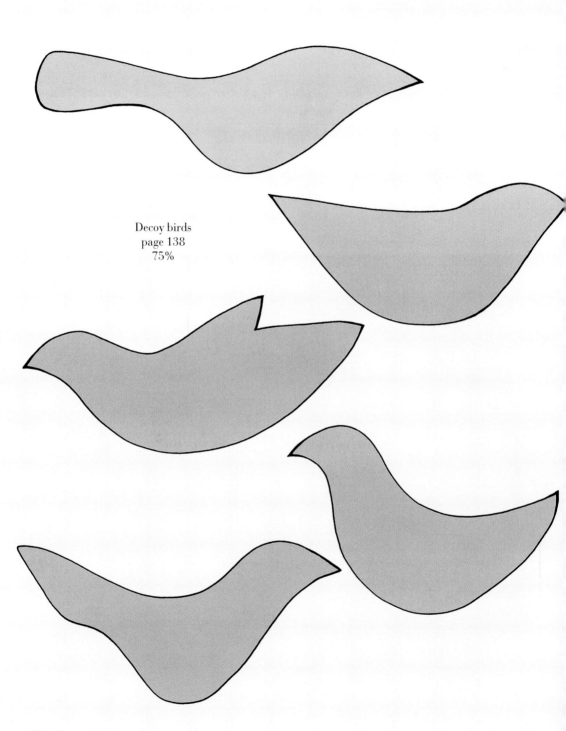

Decoy birds
page 138
75%

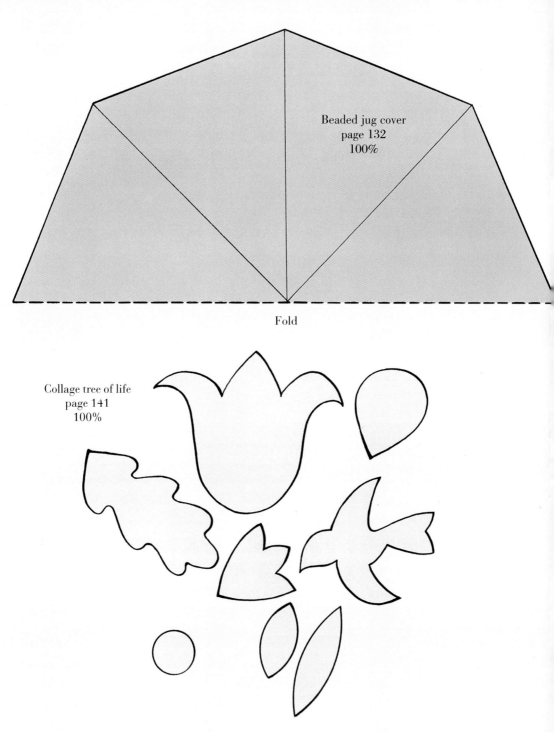

Beaded jug cover
page 132
100%

Fold

Collage tree of life
page 141
100%

Index

kitchen clock 68-9
limewashed peg rail 58-61
painted wooden box 56-7
pawprint shelves 62-4
Scandinavian door panels 54-5
tartan upholstered stool 65-7

G
gingham painted wall 22-3
glass bottle, painted 118-19
gold size, Japan 146-7
graining brush 144-5

H, I
hammers, claw 144-5
heart motif 16, 107
"Hitchcock" style 49
hooked rag rug 95-7
horse border, stamped (floor) 32-4
ink rollers 144-5
inks 72, 146-7

J, K, L
Japan gold size 146-7
jug cover, beaded 132-3
kitchen clock 68-9
knife box, rustic 110-11
lampshade, decorated 107-9
laundry basket, painted 120-1
limewashed peg rail 58-61
linen tea towel 146-7
lining brushes 144-5

M, N
masking 149
materials 14-15, 146-7
motifs and patterns 16-17
  door panel motifs 38-40

rooster cushion 83-5
  see also stamped patterns; stencils
    and stencilling
napkin, cross stitch 86-7
natural sponge 144-5

P
paint rollers 144-5
paintbrushes 144-5
painting 148
  chequerboard floor 35-7
  colour washes 10, 20
  framed memories 130-1
  gingham painted wall 22-3
  limewashed peg rail 58-61
  painted glass bottle 118-19
  painted laundry basket 120-1
  painted staircase 30-1
  painted window surround 41-3
  painted wooden box 56-7
  pawprint shelves 62-4
  rustic knife box 110-11
  Scandinavian door panels 54-5
paints 146-7
palette see colour schemes
pargeting 41
patchwork 17
squared patchwork quilt 88-91
patterns see motifs and patterns;
  stamped patterns

pawprint shelves 62-4
peg rail, limewashed 58-61
photocopy transfer, rooster cushion
  83-5
plaid patterns 16
potato prints, clover leaf tablecloth
  92-4

Q, R
quarry tiles 15
quilts
  appliqué window quilt 80-2
  squared patchwork quilt 88-91
rag rug, hooked 95-7
reclaimed timber 9, 46, 146
rolling pin holder 128-9
rooster cushion 83-5

S
sandpaper 144-5
Scandinavian door panels 54-5
scissors 144-5
sewing 72-3
  appliqué window quilt 80-2
  beaded jug cover 132-3
  cross stitch napkin 86-7
  rooster cushion 83-5
Shakers 8
shelves, pawprint 62-4
simple spongeware 112-14

ACKNOWLEDGEMENTS

The authors would like to thank the following people for their contribution to this book:
Graham Rae for his atmospheric photographs; his assistant Sarah for her hard work in the studio; Leeann Mackenzie for her sensitive styling; Mark Wood for his step-by-step photography and his assistant Edward Park; Paul Roberts for his help and expertise; Ray and Madhu McChrystal for their creativity and craftsmanship and Cathy Marriott at Anness Publishing.

The authors and publishers would like to thank the following companies who supplied products and materials for photography:
New England Direct, PO Box 5221, Bromsgrove, Worcestershire, B610BY
Grand Illusions, 2-4 Crown Road, St Margarets, Twickenham, TW1 3EE. Tel: (0181) 744 1046
Magpies, 152 Wandsworth Bridge Road, London SW6 2HH. Tel: (0171) 736 3738
Tobias and the Angel, 68 White Hart Lane, Barnes, London SW13 0PZ. Tel: (0181) 878 8902

The publishers would like to thank the following photographers and craft artists:
p12 right: photograph by Steve Tanner, p13 bottom right: object created by Mary Maguire, photo by Spike Powell, top left photo by Peter Williams; p 17 top left: object created by Lesley Stansfield, photo by Michelle Garrett, bottom: photo by Steve Tanner; p47: object created by Jonty Henshall, photo by Spike Powell; p101 top: object created by Dorothy Wood, photo by Michelle Garrett; p124 photo by Michelle Garrett.

We would like to dedicate this book to Clare Nicholson, wishing her success in the garden.

NOTES

NOTES

NOTES

NOTES

NOTES

NOTES